To the fighters, the hand-holders, the caretakers. This is for you. I see you.

Published by Simon & Schuster
New York   London   Toronto   Sydney   New Delhi

NOBODY EVER TALKS ABOUT ANYTHING BUT THE END

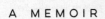

A MEMOIR

LIZ LEVINE

SIMON &
SCHUSTER
CANADA

Simon & Schuster Canada
A Division of Simon & Schuster, Inc.
166 King Street East, Suite 300
Toronto, Ontario M5A 1J3

This Simon & Schuster Canada edition January 2020

SIMON & SCHUSTER CANADA and colophon are trademarks
of Simon & Schuster, Inc.

For information about special discounts for bulk purchases,
please contact Simon & Schuster Special Sales at 1-800-268-3216
or CustomerService@simonandschuster.ca.

Illustrations by Jax Smith

Manufactured in the United States of America

10 9 8 7 6 5 4 3 2 1

Library and Archives Canada Cataloguing in Publication
    Title: Nobody ever talks about anything but the end : a memoir of loss /
by Liz Levine.
    Names: Levine, Liz, 1976– author.
    Identifiers: Canadiana (print) 20190098430 | Canadiana (ebook) 20190098457 |
ISBN 9781982109332
    (softcover) | ISBN 9781982109349 (ebook)
    Subjects: LCSH: Levine, Liz, 1976–| LCSH: Sisters—Death. | LCSH: Sisters—
Biography. | LCSH: Loss
    (Psychology) | LCSH: Grief. | LCSH: Suicide. | LCGFT: Autobiographies.
    Classification: LCC BF575.G7 L48 2019 | DDC 155.9/37—dc23

ISBN 978-1-9821-0933-2
ISBN 978-1-9821-0934-9 (ebook)

"If I succeed in ending my life tonight/this a.m. I am unsure which stories will remain of me, if any."

—TAMARA LEVINE

FOREWORD

When my best friend and first love, Judson, got sick it looked like a disease. He was quiet and listless, he lost weight, his skin looked grey, and his eyes lost their spark. His sickness and, ultimately, his death broke my heart, but it made sense to my brain. I saw the illness take him. I saw him fight it, and I saw him lose his battle. I knew I didn't have a cure for cancer and despite my best efforts, I knew I could not save him.

It wasn't like that with my sister, Tamara.

She stayed alive—and sick—for decades. But *he* died.

No one could validate her illness for me—not parents or doctors. When I first started to identify my sister as "crazy," I was told not to be mean. More to the point, I was told I was wrong. I was told to open myself more to her, to be more vulnerable and more accessible. That is good advice optically. But I was missing vital information: No one was actually aware that she *was* sick. Or that her deep, cutting cruelty came from illness.

So I opened up, and I got hurt, over and over again. And the more hurt I got, the less it became about getting to know my sister, and the more it became about trying to find the truth. Trying to fix her.

Fixing is a job for the smart and the strong. It's also the perfect escape for a sensitive soul, so that's who I pretended to be—and that stuck. So now I'm smart and strong and have survived my sister's suicide, and everyone wants to share their issues around mental health—like I might have some answers or like I might be able to fix someone. But I can't.

I wish there was an Al-Anon or PFLAG for this. Maybe then I could give some advice. But there isn't. And I can't give that advice. I did this wrong, I didn't love her right, and I can't take that back. The best I can do is try to figure out *where* I went wrong, to become a detective in death. For now, that means working in reverse. That makes sense to me because the only place I have to work with is the end.

And in this reverse engineering (in the words and the details and the act of being vulnerable with all of the information at hand) I might finally be learning what to do with all the feelings I have. Something that is productive or that might touch someone.

———————

Six weeks after my sister died, I got a tattoo on my wrist. It says *make _____*.

Eight weeks after, I wrote the first story for this book.

And I'm starting where all of us do. With the alphabet.

A

ALPHABET

I read a book called *The Lover's Dictionary* by David Levithan. And he's right: every word in the dictionary is a synonym for love.

Every word also works for loss.

ACTION

This whole book is a verb for me.

ASHES

My uncle Brian passed away in June of 2004. He requested that his body be cremated and spread across his property.

We spread the ashes. We hugged. And then we went for dinner.

It wasn't until we hit the door of the restaurant that my father noted to someone, "You've got a little Brian on your back."

ADDICTED

People always comment on how I never cry. That's not completely true. I'm rarely if never angry, but I am sensitive and easily hurt, and so I cry in that space—as in, I tear up a little. I don't cry when I'm sad, or at least I didn't for years. Somewhere along the line, that got logged in my brain as a weakness. I'm sure it started when I was five and my mother gave birth to quadruplets and one of them, my infant sister, died.

I'm sure my mother cried a lot around that time. And then the surviving triplets came home from the hospital, and they cried a lot too. Just at the time when the triplets stopped crying, my mother lost both her parents. Less than three years later, my parents got divorced. So I grew up in a sea of tears. I never wanted to contribute to the flow, for fear that all of us would drown.

It is snowing when I wake up on the morning of April 3, 2005. Judson has been dead for four days, and I have not shed a tear. I remind myself that I have survived this long through numerous losses, heartbreak, failed exams, and family drama without those tears. I seem to be fine. I lie in bed and wonder if my suit will be warm enough. Serious enough. Protective enough to wrap me in the illusion of professionalism for the bulk of the day. I am focused on practicalities.

> *Shower.*
> *Dress.*
> *Practice the eulogy while you dry your hair.*
> *Put on an empathetic smile.*
> *Keep it on all day.*

It's my turn to give the eulogy. I feel like I've waited hours in this synagogue for this moment, yet I feel panicked that it's happening so soon. I adjust the microphone and look at Judson's family—right at them. I want them to look back at me, I want to feel their pain.

I want to feel anything.

But I don't. I don't cry. My voice doesn't waver even a little bit, and I wear these truths like medals as we pile back into the car.

The cemetery is surreal: slate-grey tombstones, big fat flakes of snow. I can see Judson's father, Saul, already there: tall, in a long navy coat and hat with the snow swirling around him, standing at the foot of his son's grave.

For all the details I have already forgotten about that day and those few months, and for all those details that I never digested in the first place, what stands alone is this image.

I am too cheerful at the cemetery. Greeting people, giving hugs, staying warm by moving around, staying distracted. I'm 29, and my mom still gives me "the eye"—it says, *Settle down, look around you, is this behaviour appropriate?*

What is appropriate at this moment? Every time I move, my boots make a deafening crunch in the snow. I know I should stand still, pay attention, pay respects, but if I do I'll start to *feel*.

In retrospect, I can sense the tension between how much I needed to feel and how much I didn't want to. And now I know that it took Judson dying for me to even realize that I had feelings. And it wasn't the death itself, or the funeral obviously, it was the years that came after that were the most revealing. It's about the moment I realized, *I can't avoid feeling any longer.*

I don't know when the breaking point was, or if there was an aha moment at all. I just started crying sometimes. Always by myself. And then I started laughing a little harder too. I began to realize that I can *feel* and that the act of feeling, feeling anything at all, is amazing.

I've become addicted to feeling, addicted to the sensation of awe. I seek it out. Mushroom trips, magical adventures, dangerous relationships, and deep, heady conversations. And it turns out, I am good at feeling things—like, really good.

I only wish I'd known about feeling from the start. I wish someone had told me that vulnerability is like a superpower, if handled with care.

But life taught me the opposite.

B

BEGINNING

The point in time or space at which something starts.

The first part of something.

The part that comes after the end.

BRIEF (HISTORY OF DEATH)

Death: It's about what you are left with.

Who: Katherine, my sister.
How: Illness? Infanticide?
Residue: People die. People die before they get to live. Babies die. Babies get killed.

Who: Gammy.
How: Lung cancer.
Residue: My mother took me to visit Gammy after her first round of chemo. I was eight, and I wasn't prepared to see her. She was skinny and bald, like someone out of an alien movie. I know I spent lots of time with her—I remember the apartment full of knickknacks not for children, and I remember the small stuffed knitted orange bear I kept at her place—but this vision is now the only living image of her I can recall.

Who: Gramps.
How: He died six months after Gammy, of "natural causes."
Residue: He was my favourite. I miss him. I am haunted by the idea that someone can die of a broken heart.

Who: I think her name was Kim. She was in my Grade 3 class.
How: Her father came home from work one day and lost it. He

pulled out a gun and shot her mother in plain sight. Kim grabbed her little brother to protect him, and her father shot her in the back and then shot himself.

Residue: The little brother.

Who: Jonathan, who went to the boys' school down the street. I think we were 13.

How: Went out into the backyard after breakfast in his school uniform, put his father's gun in his mouth, and pulled the trigger.

Residue: I understand that it is possible not just to be killed but to kill yourself.

Who: Casey, a girl in my brother's Grade 2 class.

How: They told us she died of a broken heart when her big brother left town for university.

Residue: I am re-haunted by the idea that someone can die from a broken heart.

Who: Wendy from the ski team.

How: Skied into a tree in junior team qualifiers and broke her neck on impact.

Residue: I stopped going so fast.

Who: Greg and Chris, friends from high school.

How: Drunk-driving accident.

Residue: I started going fast again.

Who: My friend Natalie's mom.

How: A brain aneurysm the night of our high school play.

Residue: The sound Natalie made when they told her backstage.

Who: Judson, my first love and best friend.

How: Burkitt's leukemia.
Residue: Life is about loss.

Who: Tamara, my sister.
How: Suicide; she jumped.
Residue: All the things.

BROTHERS

I have three of them. You should know them all.

Peter was always my favourite growing up. He is gentle and sensitive in a way only he and I share in the family. And he can make anyone laugh. In retrospect, I think this was his way of easing the tension that so often existed in our household.

At the cottage one summer, Mom herded us all up from the lake so she could get dinner ready. There was the usual cacophony of complaints and whines and "just five more minutes," so by the time we climbed the 200 steps back up to the cottage there were some grumpy faces in the mix and everyone disappeared to their own corner of the cabin to mope and regroup alone. Minutes ticked by in near silence before we heard a voice from the basement: Peter's sweet little voice. We all scrambled downstairs to find him sitting in the oversized laundry sink, rain boots on, legs splayed out over the edge, paddling with an abandoned canoe paddle and singing at the top of his voice, "Yes, we have no bananas."

This is his way. Humour. And sensitivity.

Years later, we were driving down the Don Valley Parkway in Toronto. Mom had picked up each of us from our after-school activity of choice and was racing the light in the gathering dusk and aiming to have dinner for four kids on the table, stat. Peter piped up from the back of the car that we had just driven by a pigeon on the road that looked injured and could Mom turn the car around and rescue it? Her answer: "Absolutely not." It was quiet for a moment, and then Peter's sweet little voice began to sing "All Things Bright and Beautiful." Mom grimaced and turned the car around . . .

Alexis was different. He was stronger, more assertive, and always had a fierce independent streak. He always said what he meant and meant what he said. As a child, he changed his given name from James Alexander to Alexis. It was simple for him: he liked it better. He works his universe like this—bending it to his wishes. When he was older, he would storm out of the house when Mom tried to ground him, and by the time I left home for university, the triplets were barely 16 but Alexis had already started his own business and was running around with a pager that he prioritized like a heart surgeon on call.

Alexis, who I now call Lex, went to the same university as me, and it was in our year of crossover there that we really connected. He would escape residence to come sit on my floor and hang out with my friends. He was awkward and nerdy and always had the front pockets of his dress pants overstuffed with his wallet and keys and notepads and anything else he wanted to carry around. But he liked being around the older kids, and frankly, we liked him. Lex became not just my brother, but my friend. A friend I would choose were we not already related.

Over this same time, Peter seemed to slip away from us. He went out east for university, and while there, he went from being an outgoing, funny, and self-admitted "player" to a quiet, near reclusive man. And as the last decade has gone by, he has adopted what is, to Lex and me, a fairly extreme worldview and a set of political and religious beliefs that have severed him from us further. We miss him.

Finally, there is little Joshy. My brother with the same name as Judson's brother. Mom brought him home when we were all at university. And I mean literally just brought him home. She met him on a case she was handling for her work at the Children's Aid Society. He came from a tough background and a broken home, and my mother felt it high time to raise a child who really needed her—so she offered to foster him.

We were all charmed by Joshy immediately. He was bad. Don't underestimate me—REALLY BAD. Mouthy, volatile, a product of his upbringing. The first day I met him, I stepped through the door of the family home, suitcase and laundry in hand, to find this tiny, precocious child, age six, standing at the top of the stairs, hand on his hip, shoulders thrown back, fiercely telling my stepfather, Allan, "Kiss my butt, bitch." And I fell instantly in love with his big blue eyes and Harry Potter spectacles combined with all the naive ferocity and failings that years in the system had granted him. Our hearts melted, and he became one of us.

There were three sisters too.

Now I'm the only one.

BREAK

By the spring of 2014, Tamara got offered a job with Save the Children in Australia. I think in her mind—which was getting sicker by the day—the job was a solution. She was going to get away from home, away from the people who were worried about her and telling her she was sick. Away from everything: from the flashing lights and the people following her, from the email hacking and the mind machine interface of her psychotic waking dreams.

The rest of us weren't sure that being thousands of miles away, literally on the other side of the world, was the best plan, but Momma Bear was prepared to support her—as she always did, with all of us. Tamara gave up her apartment and sold or stored everything she owned, even her car. She moved in with Mom for the last two months before her travels. In the weeks before she left, she asked Mom to borrow the family car for a night so she could make a trip north of the city to say goodbye to some friends.

At 3 a.m. that night/morning after Tamara left, Mom got a call from the police in Belleville, Ontario, the opposite direction from Aurora, which was where Tamara said she was going. It would be the first of many calls that my mother would receive from police over the next two years. Apparently, they had pulled Tamara over, and she rambled on with a crazy story about being told to follow an ambulance. She was so incoherent that the cops thought she was on drugs.

Mom didn't tell me this story then. She rarely told me these stories. She felt that they just added ammunition to what she perceived to be my dislike of Tamara. Instead, she continued to outwardly support Tamara on her journey, and encouraged us to support her and say loving goodbyes.

I didn't know it then, but that goodbye WAS important. After Tamara's eventual psychotic break, she would never be the same again.

Two weeks later, in early June 2014, Tamara left for Australia. She was nervous and had started obsessing about her perceived role in the Malaysia Airlines crash earlier that spring. She felt responsible for friends dying in plane crashes, for random fires that started in other parts of the city, and, by the time she landed in Australia, she was convinced that she had been abducted in an airport en route and force-fed nuts.

That was one of the few things Tamara and I had in common: a nut allergy. And so, as with all her stories, the fiction (being poisoned) had a grain of truth (the allergy).

She told these tales to Lex and me via Facebook Messenger. The conversations were hard to follow not just because of the ideas but because of how her mind processed them. Her thoughts jumped all over the place, moving from the middle of one saga to the end of another to the beginning of the previous. Sometimes she was confessing to us, and other times she was accusing us of being part of the "conspiracy."

I tried to tell Mom once again how sick I thought Tamara was. I tried to keep up with the diatribes on Messenger. I tried. And then I didn't. Then I got on a plane for Los Angeles and spent the summer in the hot sunshine with my friends, developing film and television projects and believing that everything would be OK.

Lex called me in August, freaked-out. He told me that Tamara had been terminated from her job for reasons unknown but that from what he could discern it had something to do with lying about being HIV positive and ordering antiviral drugs. Apparently, there was a bizarre insurance claim, and Save the Children wanted their relocation fees back.

All that was insane enough, but none of it was the reason Lex was really disturbed. Tamara had reached out the day before online to tell him she had lost her job but was going to travel for a couple of weeks to take advantage of being in Australia. Then she would come home. But the next morning, she was already back in Toronto and had left a package at Lex's front door with gifts for the kids. The kids he was trying to protect from her.

So Lex reached out and agreed to meet Tamara at a restaurant, far away from his home and his children. He told Tamara she was "not in her right mind," and that she should check in to a hospital. She finally agreed, and he hoped it was the start of the cure.

Later that day, my mother called. "Tamara isn't well," she said.

It was the call I had been waiting over a decade to receive.

There it was: hope.

Now Mom would fight for her.

Now that her psychotic break had happened, we were finally all on the same page.

Now it would get better.

C

CANCER

A serious disease caused by cells that are not normal and that can spread to one or many parts of the body.

The fourth sign of the zodiac, which comes between Gemini and Leo and has a crab as its symbol.

CHLORINE

I've been told that Judson and I met at a swim meet. I'm sure that is true, but I don't remember which meet. It doesn't matter anyway—the Truth changes after someone dies; the relationship changes. There is no one to confirm your tales, but no one to deny them either. The relationship that lives in your head is actually the only one that exists.

I associate my early teen years with the smell of chlorine, with the echo of the swimming pool, the churning of my prerace stomach and my hair frozen into icicles as Judson and I walked home together. Hand in hand, flirting with pneumonia and love. He was my thirteen-year-old "love affair" (meaning we kissed but mostly just held hands and talked). And he changed me.

He was so tall—even back then, he was over 6'4". I liked the way he bobbed his head down towards me to show that he was listening, and I liked his big blue eyes that said more than even his fast-talking mouth. He had giant hands, and when he took mine in his, my hand would disappear into his glove, and I would be warm even in the biting 20 below. I don't know if I was too young to feel the cold back then or if I just didn't notice the bitter winds. Most nights we said our goodbyes on the corner one block from my house and two from his. It was all snow-jacket hugs and runny-nose kisses and the obligations of family dinner.

He was the first person I remember talking with—not talking to, or about, or being talked at—but the first person who heard me. We talked a lot about swimming, competition, and our siblings. How much we loved and hated them. We talked about Tamara. He understood, but also, he didn't. Because I didn't, and my parents didn't. We talked about our parents—our fathers, lawyers, and our mothers, mine a psychologist and his in real estate. We talked about how they shaped us, if we would be them when we grew up, about what it meant to be the eldest and what it did to us. Would we be better adults as a result, more equipped for the "real world"?

Our conversations took days. To school, through spare periods and lunch breaks, on long telephone calls, at the pool and all the way home. Sometimes we were focused on one idea or one conversation for weeks on end. Other times we would have six conversations on the go, all at varying stages that would weave in and out of our daily existence like the air we breathed. Slamming locker doors at lunch to get out to the lawn and make that point that had been sitting in my head since we parted before first bell. Picking up the phone as soon as family dinner was cleared to add some detail or ask some question. We even had the occasional midnight visit—whispering under the light on his front porch or mine, when the next thought (one I could not remember now if my life depended on it) could not wait until the following morning.

We talked about ideas. I learned that the things that were stuck in my head were not stupid. Sometimes they were cool or smart. I was addicted to ideas, to my first brush with wonder and awe. I learned that he had stuff like that in his head too. I learned that it was endlessly fascinating to just gaze into his big blue eyes. I could have done that forever. I learned to give space to let people be who they are, and I learned about the size of the human heart.

Our parents were thrilled—although they didn't tell us that then. This was IT. IT was part of the package: the Private School, the University Degree, the Career Success, the Marriage, the Children, and the Fulfilling Retirement on not-for-profit boards.

They would cluck with feigned concern when we were late for dinner or curfew. My mother would often remind me that it was OK to "date," but when anyone else showed up at the door she'd ask, "Where's Judson?" Our fathers worked in the same law firm. Our mothers went to the same PTA meetings. Our younger brothers were the same age. If I was ever going to marry the Jewish doctor of my father's dreams, this had to be IT.

But IT wasn't. We were just kids, after all.

It was easy, though. We weren't really alive then. I don't remember us thinking, or fighting, or forming identities beyond the ones we were given, but it doesn't mean we weren't happy. We didn't have reason to take sides because life was long. It was forever. We were still safe and swimming. Following the black line at the bottom of the pool—straight ahead to the finish.

He was a lifeguard that first summer that we were together. He worked in High Park. It was all the way west on the Bloor Street subway line. He wore a red tank top with LIFEGUARD in bold white letters and red shorts. He looked important in that lifeguard chair, and that made *me* feel important. I could feel it from the moment I stepped onto the subway, looking out at the world with my Walkman playing in my ears.

I am going to see my BOYFRIEND.

He is a LIFEGUARD.

He SAVES LIVES.

Where are you going?

One day I got to the pool and he was behind the lifeguard shed, pacing. I thought he might be sneaking a cigarette. We flirted with cigarettes then. But he wasn't smoking.

It was all an accident, and it was not his fault. Of course, fault rarely determines impact. It would change his life. And mine.

There are a lot of rules to shift change at the pool—you have to climb down from the lifeguard chair while the replacement guard stands beside it and watches the pool. Then you have to watch the pool while your replacement climbs into the chair. Once everyone on deck is replaced, a whistle blows and the guards off shift can take a break. But that day someone looked away or laughed with a friend. Any good lifeguard knows that it only takes a moment for a head to slip under the surface, that the splashing of other swimmers and the glaring sun can make it almost impossible to see the bottom of the pool from the lifeguard chair.

According to the paramedics, the kid was on the bottom of the pool for two minutes before Judson saw him and pulled him out. Judson had stretched him out on the deck and frantically began pumping his chest, forcing his own panicked breath in to the child's lungs, trying to make his heart beat or lungs breathe. His body must have felt so fragile compared to the plastic blue dummies at lifeguard training. I wondered what it sounded like when Judson broke the boy's ribs performing CPR. He said it was nothing like the synthetic cracking sound that the dummies make. It must have felt soft. The paramedics said it was only three minutes, but it must have seemed like hours before they arrived and pulled Judson away. Off the body.

So he was shaking behind the guard shed when I arrived. EMS later explained that the shaking was leftover from the rush of adrenaline. They kept Judson about half an hour and then told us to go. The pool was closed until further notice.

We took the subway home. I tried to hold his hand, but he pulled it away. He didn't want to be comforted. I understood this somehow. We went to his house and waited by the phone for the news. The boy died before he reached the ER. And with him, the innocence of that first summer job, when work meant sunshine and pocket change. We knew that we had never taken the job seriously until then, that we had not really taken *anything* seriously, not love or even life.

So we became serious.

We over-thought everything. He had tried to save someone. He had touched someone who was dead, dying. Maybe he had touched him in the moment of death. This conversation lasted for almost two months. What was the moment of death like? Was it wonderful or terrifying? Did that kid know he was dying in those moments? Does anyone?

That summer we both started thinking. But we were thinking small for the first time since we had met. We were being reactive to death. Living in spite of it.

This just served to reinforce the idea that my parents, power lawyer father and superhero shrink mother, made über kids, built of Teflon. I will not cry, I will not crack, I can withstand anything.

The world was not a fair place, and we knew it. Our new personalities hung out on Frybrook Road during lunch break and smoked cigarettes in our spare periods. We drank under the bridge in Sir Winston Churchill Park. We made out in public. To the rest of the world we were teenagers, but to us . . . we were taking shape, and taking shape together.

I remember kissing Judson under that bridge. I remember he always smelled like chlorine back then.

CHRISTMAKUH

By blood, we are Jews. By upbringing and education, we are Anglican. By tradition, we try everything.

My mom is remarried—her husband, Allan, has two children of his own, both of them married, and my stepbrother has three kids. My father is also remarried—his wife, Donna, has four children, most of them married, and many of them have kids.

This makes the holiday planning in our world more than a little bit confusing, and our traditions confounding to most. But in the end, things are the same as in most families: food, laughter, and a little bit of drama and eggshell walking.

The setup looks similar every year, but, in 2011, there was this slew of emails.

> To: Dad, Dawn, Liz, Pete, Tamara
> From: Lex
> Date: December 13, 2011
>
> For anyone who hasn't yet got this on their calendar, I've been nominated to send out a reminder and/or first notice about a holiday dinner with Dad before he and Donna go south.

The date is December 20th, which also happens to be the first night of Chanukah.

As such, we were thinking that we could perhaps have everybody (significant others included of course) by our new place at 6:30 p.m. to light the first candle of Chanukah (in the glow of our Christmas tree, no less). Then we could go on to dinner from there. Also, instead of an uberfancy restaurant, we were thinking about something a bit more casual this year.

So, in that spirit, we're asking you to vote for one of the following dinner options on the Danforth:

1. *I would like to have a traditional Jewish meal, and so I pick Chinese Food*
2. *Since we are on the Danforth, we should eat Greek Food*
3. *I would prefer to have something healthy, and so I would like Sushi*
4. *I think that this whole idea is stupid and crazy and I want to have a fight about it.*

Please pick from choices 1 to 4 above and email a response. If no option receives 50% of the vote or more, we will have a run off. Couples get one combined vote, or a 0.5 vote each, and Dad breaks any ties.

Lex

Which led to the following slew of responses, the first from Lex's wife, Dawn:

I'm a "when in Rome" kinda girl . . . I choose Greek.

Xoxo
Dawn

I'm a "when on the Danforth" kinda girl . . . So I choose Greek too!

L

Well, I'm with Pete. We need to get back to our roots. Chinese food is my vote.

So we are at 1.5 for Greek, 1.5 for Chinese, 0 for Sushi. Tamara, you get to break the tie.

Lex

Can't I vote? As to our Chinese roots, there were in fact four different waves of Jews in to China:

1. *The Silk Road ending in Kaifung*
2. *1841—the settlement of Shanghai by the Hardoons (HSBC) and the Sassoons (British East India Company)—think opium and read your cousin, David Rotenberg's book—Shanghai*
3. *The Russian Revolution*
4. *The Holocaust*

History lesson over.

Much love,
Dad

Stop trying to rob Tamara of her moment in the sun here!
Dad, you only get to vote if, following the votes of all

eligible children, there is a tie. At this stage, a tie could only result if one of the following occurs (a) Tamara votes for Sushi, (b) Tamara votes for #4, (c) Tamara introduces a significant other, and they split their votes evenly between Chinese and Greek, or (d) Tamara elects not to vote.

Lex

Hi,

    I am tempted to chose option 4 (what would a Levine family gathering be like if I didn't add a little spice and melodrama to the mix) . . .

Ta

CATALYST

It has become a matter of fact to me: anxiety leads to paranoia, and paranoia can lead to delusions.

My mother always said that my leaving Tamara out of things made Tamara more anxious. I don't think I left her out much more than the average older, irritated sibling of triplets would. But still . . .

I wonder if it's all my fault.

CHURCH

It's Christmas Eve, one month after my sister's suicide, and my mother needs a magic moment right now, more than she ever has. I pride myself on the ability to construct these moments. To have the split-second sense that I can alter the fabric of the universe, change the energy of a space or of a group of people, for the better. It's the only kind of magic I believe in.

We are going to church tonight. Tamara used to go with Mom every year, and Lex and I would roll our eyes and make jokes about Jews bursting into flame. Not this year. This year, Tamara is still barely in the ground. This year, we can't make fun. This year, we will just go. Silent, well behaved, and we will stand on either side of Mom with our arms around her and sing Christmas carols if that is what will make her happy.

It sounds easy enough. But looks can be deceiving. Lex hosted Christmas Eve at his place forty-five minutes away. And it's snowing. And it's not easy to get a four-year-old and a two-year-old to sleep when Santa is coming. And there is NEVER parking at Grace Church-on-the-Hill on Christmas Eve. But by some amazing stroke of Christmas luck, or maybe just a reprieve from the more terrible "luck" we have been having, we find a spot less than a block away.

It's magic, I guess, but not magic enough and nowhere close to fairy dust we actually need right now to make this Christmas possible.

My brother pulls right up to the car in front, and I ask, "What if we want to leave early and the guy behind parks too close? Mom is going to want to leave early. Seriously, just give us some room." He shrugs, and I don't fight it. I'm not up for battling with the lawyer tonight.

The church is lovely now that we aren't ridiculing it. It feels still here, even with all the people. And I'm reminded that I like Christmas carols. But all of this niceness doesn't seem to be helping Mom. In fact, it's kind of breaking her.

She is coming apart between us during the service and people around us can tell. We have been here an hour, and as congregants begin to have communion, she suggests that we, the heathens, slip out. As we pass through the church doors and reach the coat rack at the back of the church, she starts to cry again. "We didn't get to light the candles. It always happens at the end, and I want to light one for her."

I leave Lex to help her with her coat and walk back through the doors. The basket of candles is placed mid-aisle, and I don't even think twice. I walk up the aisle in my red ski jacket, take three candles, and then turn and walk back out. All eyes in the church on me.

I hold the the candles out to Mom and Lex as we go out the doors onto the steps. It's not a cold night per se, given that it's December 24th in Toronto. I pull a lighter out of my pocket. For the first time ever, my mother doesn't ask me why I have a lighter on me.

And standing on those steps of the church she has been coming to with my sister for 35 years, we light the candles. Lex watches the wind flirt with the flames and cups his hands around them to keep them lit, like it matters.

"See, Sweet-pea?" my mother says. "We all came here together for you. And you could've been here. If you'd just hung on a little longer." Her voice breaks. "If you weren't such a bum, we'd be having Christmas now." She cries. We hug her.

It's a moment between us. One we need. And for all the pain and insanity that all of this is, I feel a flicker of pride. I make these moments. Always. And now, now I have my hand on that tiny corner of the fabric of the universe, and Lex can feel it too, the energy that can be changed in this space.

And then it is over. We walk back to the car. As we get there, we see that someone has parked less than two inches from Lex's back bumper. It is going to be impossible to get the car out. I nudge him to look. He pauses, grimaces, and then says, "Goddam proctologist," and muses, "If only someone could have foreseen this."

CONDOLENCES

Everyone has that friend. The person who asks you about the things you don't want to talk about but probably should talk about. I am drawn to those people. I guess they remind me of my mother. I met France a year before Tamara died. It was instantaneous. Soul sister. And her sister was sick too, in very similar ways to Tamara. France and I spent a lot of time talking about our sisters.

It's 5:30 a.m., and my mother has just told me that Tamara died. I hang up the phone and send a couple of texts—just a select few. Less than 10 minutes later, my phone rings in my hand, and it's France. She says she felt me. She says, "Get. Here. Now."

She opens the door when I arrive, already in tears, arms open. My first instinct is relief. And then, at a loss for what comes next, she says, "At least my sister would have called me first."

Before the words are out of her mouth, she regrets them. Her hands over her mouth. Horrified.

I am instantly wounded. But before I can even feel how badly the words sting, we are instantly in laughter and then in tears, and she is instantly forgiven.

I'm so sorry.
Our warmest condolences,
She's in a better place.
At least she's not in pain now.
She's in our prayers.
Take comfort in knowing _____ (insert any of the above three statements here).
With heartfelt condolences,
I understand how you feel.
I've been there.
I'm so sorry for your loss.
Deepest sympathies.
We are very saddened by this loss.
My heart goes out to you.
Our deepest condolences,
Words cannot begin to express our sadness.
Our love to you and your family at this time.
I am here for you.
Take comfort in your memories.
You are in my thoughts.
Our thoughts and prayers are with you.
We are thinking of you.
We are thinking of you during this difficult time.
With deepest sympathy,
My sincere sympathy,
Remember that we love and care about you.
With caring thoughts,
With loving memories,
Our hearts go out to you in your time of sorrow.
She will remain in our hearts forever.
We send you thoughts of comfort.
Please accept our most heartfelt sympathies for your loss . . .

our thoughts are with you and your family during this difficult time.

With love and hugs,

We will miss her,

Remembering you and her in our minds and in our hearts.

We send you thoughts of peace and courage.

We are here to support you in your grieving process.

With sincere sympathy,

We will never forget her.

May your heart and soul find peace and comfort.

Peace, Prayers and Blessings,

Wishing you peace to bring comfort, courage to face the days ahead.

Wishing you loving memories to forever hold in your hearts.

I don't have the words to express my sadness for you . . .

———————————

And in all this white noise of nothingness I realize that, as it turns out, France's response was the most memorable and authentic condolence I received. Because I heard beneath it how horrified she was and how deeply she felt my pain. And her own.

"At least my sister would have called me first." She is willing for this to be true.

D

DEATH-IVERSARY

I remember them better than anniversaries.

DAWN

Lex tells me I first met my sister-in-law, Dawn, in June 2009. Apparently, they were in Vancouver for a Liberal Party convention and they met me for lunch. I don't remember that day: where we ate lunch, what I thought of her when I first saw her or heard her voice.

But I don't remember life without Dawn. It's like she has always been there.

Familiar. Familial. Family.

Another sister.

I didn't know she'd be the only one. But she's definitely the one I would choose.

DYNASTY

According to my father, everyone we are related to and, moreover, everyone we know, can be traced back to a shtetl in Poland. I'm not sure if this is truth, or urban myth, or something my father has willed into being, but some days it sure seems like he's right. We are related to everyone.

It's not a wonder, really: my paternal grandfather was the youngest of ten, and his wife the second youngest of five. On my mother's side, each grandparent had six siblings. So when you factor in marriages, divorces, and children, there are a LOT of cousins.

My family, it seems, with my limited historical gaze, has always lived in extremes. Both my grandfathers were type A, ambitious, and wildly successful. But also, I've learned that approximately eight of my relatives have taken their own lives. I asked my father about this, and he said, "Really smart, and really fucking crazy, on both sides of the family."

And it seems to have landed with my parents too. Both are at the top of their fields and still determined to accomplish more as they pass 70. And the boys and I are no exception. Nor was Tamara. She was brilliant.

It turns out that of the relatives who took their own lives, approximately six of them jumped (not including Tamara). One of them jumped just down the street from Tamara. Same street. Same action. Fifty years apart.

Maybe, like ambition, it just runs in the blood.

DISTRACTION

Judson came by my house every Christmas. He'd charm my mother with a basket of goodies from his parents and a brilliant smile. I would stand by awkwardly. Mom would lounge, her hip against the front hall table, her arms gently crossed, smiling easily. He matched her ease and made her laugh. Then he'd peck her on the cheek with an "I'll have her back in no time," and we'd be out the door before she could respond.

Christmas at my house was intense. We were constantly on alert for a Tamara outburst, and we had to work gently around Mom's need to control every minute—to make it perfect. Christmas at everyone's house is probably pretty intense. The living room was a hive of frenetic energy in the morning. We stepped nervously, skittish, trying to avoid family land mines, and as a result, I have never liked Christmas. I got to sleep the night before knowing that Judson would come ring my doorbell. He came to free me from the stifling family traditions that gave me the sense of being trapped in the house with Tamara. He came to plan for our annual friends Jewbouree on December 26th. And as a result we formed our own tradition around a much-needed smoke and a moment of sanity. We would walk in the cold winter air, he would bring me a gift, he would make me laugh, he would ease the pressure.

Judson did not come by last year, or the year before, when he was sick, and he would not be coming by this year. So when the doorbell rang this Christmas and I answered it . . .

. . . the world stopped.

It took a moment to understand that this was not him. He had to lean forward and put his hand on my arm. He bowed his head a little, just like Judson used to, in order to look me in the eye.

Mirage.

Looking at Judson's brother, Josh, was like getting my heart ripped out. They look so much alike, the way they both tilt their heads to one side when they are really listening, the way they laugh with their broad smiles and perfect teeth, heads tossed back, invested in the moment.

People tiptoe around Josh now, but not my mother. She wants to know how he is doing, how the pain feels right now. Almost three years have passed. "The pain never lessens; it just happens less often," she tells him as he stands in the doorway at Christmas. She is leaning her hip against the front hall table, smiling gently. Josh and I stand at the door, uncomfortable. Without Judson to charm for both of us, we feel lost.

It is an awkward extrication process . . . and as we move down the street, it is with a familiar, though not comfortable, silence. "Sorry, I just didn't know what to say to your mom," he admits.

"Yeah, neither did I. Me talk pretty one day."

He smiles—a little.

"David Sedaris," I tell him. And there are no other words, nothing left to say that has not already been said. I put my arm through his, and we turn towards his home, Judson's home, the duplex just a few blocks away.

There are no empties stacked outside the door as Josh unlocks it and we step inside. After university and some world travel, Judson returned and claimed the basement suite as his own. It has its own door to the outside with a little sheltered area for joint smoking.

I throw my jacket down on the couch, still familiar but not comfortable. I roll a joint on the glass coffee table; it feels like the thousandth time. I cut us each a line of cocaine. Josh turns on the TV. I think we are watching *Family Guy*.

Less sober, I make my way down the narrow hallway to the bathroom. On the way back, I cannot help but look—Judson's bedroom door is slightly ajar. I imagine that his mother, Kathy, feels the need to catch a glimpse each time she walks by, that the door is left open to give the semblance of life in the space behind it. As soon as I step through the door, I know that only Kathy comes in here. She sits on his bed and she cries. I check back out the door to make sure Josh is not watching. I'm not sure why it matters.

Inside is like a parallel universe where Judson is still here, still alive. Junk is piled on his desk: more unopened mail, a few cables, his cell phone . . . It is still the same as it was. And if his room is still the same, then he should still be here, no?

I open the closet to find his clothes still folded as they were left. I run my fingers over the orange sweater and bury my face in the stack of T-shirts. I stand like that, arms over my head, clutching whatever material my hands have landed on, fighting tears. Something I don't do. But in this moment I do. And it's a good thing too, because in an instant Josh is behind me.

"You should take it," he tells me, gesturing to what I have clutched in my hands. I don't even know what I'm holding on to.

"Time for another line?" one of us suggests. Probably me. We get a little higher. We watch some more *Family Guy* and then sports updates. Josh is obsessed with sports.

Once I am sure my family is in bed and we are down to a line or two each, I know it is time to go. A bump for the road, and Josh puts Judson's scarf in my hands and says, "Don't forget this."

I take Judson's scarf with me when I leave. It is the one he is wearing in the picture we all have of him. It was taken in Montreal when Judson was at McGill. He is standing on the hill with the whole city beneath his arms, which are stretched out like a raptor's. Karina, Jud's "fag hag," sidekick, and childhood friend, printed and framed the pictures for his friend Tyler and me. Maybe she made them for the family. I know she kept one for herself. I keep mine in my home office in Vancouver, tucked behind some books, where only I can see it.

I wrap the scarf around my neck, and I can smell him, I think I can, just a hint of him, his cologne, the scent of something familiar. It is snowing as I walk home wrapped up in him.

DUMB

I found a video online in 2012 that I loved so much I sent it to everyone, Tamara included. A PSA that has racked up millions of views. It was originally made to promote safety for a train station in Melbourne. It's an animated sing-along called "Dumb Ways to Die," and in it a series of adorable animated characters die in ridiculous ways and then are all delightfully brought back to life in their mangled states to sing a rousing rendition of the very catchy chorus.

Don't take my word for it. Look it up on YouTube. I guarantee you'll be singing it all night.

On November 20, 2015, Tamara sends me a message through Facebook Messenger that says, *This video has a whole new meaning now*, and has a link to "Dumb Ways to Die."

What do you mean? I ask.

I wish you peace, she says.

I wish you peace too but I still have no idea what the "whole new meaning" is behind the safety video . . .

LOL, she writes. *Sending you love. Family is family.*

I was the dumb one. I know the answer now. She was thinking about all the dumb ways she could die at that point. One year before her suicide.

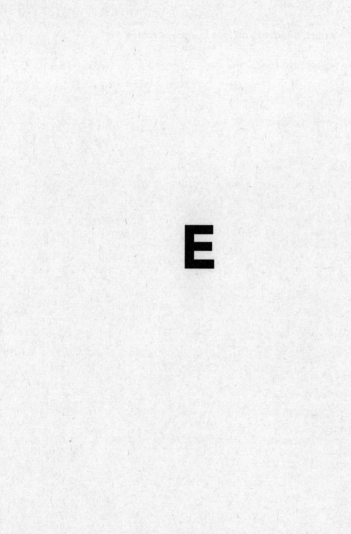

E

EASTER BUNNY

I'm an evidence-based creature at this, the ripe old age of 6. I'm the first of my friends to stop believing in the Easter Bunny, Santa Claus, and the tooth fairy, and by the time I am 8, I'm already over the Loch Ness Monster and unicorns. I pride myself on this.

I'm 10 when I stop believing in my sister for the first time. My parents have been divorced for 4 years and are continuously working with each other and all 4 kids to make this as good as possible. My sister, Tamara, aged 7 now, is working against the whole plan. Tamara tells my mother stories about my father's dating life. She tells my father stories about my mother's dating life. They all stem from a grain of truth, but to my already attentive ears, they sound like lies.

I'm 13 when the high school principal pulls me into her office to ask if my father is touching me, and where. He isn't! And so this question is like being asked when the aliens had landed or when I last saw the Easter Bunny. I sit stunned in front of her, mortified. It turns out Tamara has told her this, not because it is true but, in her words, "Because I wanted to see what would happen."

As the years go by, the illness gets worse and, to my eyes, increasingly obvious. Tamara makes plans with friends we never see, and in this era before Facebook, we can't even confirm that they exist.

There is always a boyfriend or three that we never meet and an event she's going to that doesn't seem to be actually happening.

I'm 22 and driving home to spend Christmas with the family. By this point, Tamara has become obsessed with gift giving. Our gifts are complex baskets filled with myriad things that reflect her understanding of us. This year, I got everything from movie tickets to cool pens and a small black-and-white ceramic cookie jar with the word *shrooms* tiled on the front of it. I guess this is my university undergrad reputation.

I'm 29 when I fly home to Toronto and learn that Tamara has shaved her head and is telling the whole family that she is dying of cancer. Evidence-based creature that I am, I instantly disbelieve it. Mere blocks away, Judson is actually dying of cancer, so I know what it looks like. And Tamara, she still has her eyebrows and eyelashes! I don't know yet that Tamara's disease gives her an irrational sense of responsibility for any tragedy that she's heard about. I don't connect her lie to my experience yet. So I lose any flicker of remaining belief I might have in unicorns, leprechauns, and magic, and my brother and I decide to take very practical action. We scream at my parents, we try a family intervention, we try and contact her "friends." Nothing works.

I'm 31 when Lex, the lawyer and politico who counts every black mark as a failure and every success as a résumé builder, is given a foster child for Christmas. The small child's name is Maluki, and he lives in a little village somewhere in Africa. My sister has covered his expenses for a year, and this promises to bring Maluki and his village a clean well for drinking water and some basic tools for education.

It's almost three months past Christmas when my brother's phone rings. It is a representative from Foster Parents Plan Canada. None of Maluki's bills have been paid, there is no fresh water in his village, and he is still starving to death. Lex is officially a delinquent foster dad. Apologetic and mortified beyond belief, my brother hangs up and calls Tamara. Tamara is instantly apologetic. "There must be some confusion here, they have my credit card, I'll call and sort it out, you don't need to worry about it."

It's late summer when Lex's phone rings again with a representative from Foster Parents Plan Canada on the other end of the line. Maluki is being taken away from my brother. He has failed as a parent, and he hasn't even had his own children yet. Maluki will be given to a set of parents that can handle the responsibility and prioritize saving the lives of children. My brother is crushed.

Tamara's conversations are getting stranger. Now, in the modern world of social networks, we can see her friends online and watch their exchanges. She still seems to have friends that don't exist, and she makes plans that never happen. She talks obsessively about a man named Scott Willis. Willis is a world traveller, a well-educated, handsome man living somewhere in Denmark with a name like an American spy. And he loves her, and they are best friends, and he will fly across the world for her if she needs it. And Lex and I believe in him about as much as we do in the Easter Bunny.

In these last two years, Tamara's disease gets so bad that it finally gets named: psychotic with paranoid delusions. Her conversations go from secret meetings with the president and her email being tracked, all the way to tinfoil hats and alien invasions. Life becomes a mess of psych wards and doctors and pills and medication. And then she jumps from her 29th-floor balcony to her death.

Lex and I manage the family through the funeral. He gives the eulogy. And as soon as the service is over, we sneak away out a side door for a cigarette. I'm just absorbing the quiet and trying to wrap my head around all this before I have to go hug a thousand strangers. We are standing quietly, hidden around the side of the funeral home, when a young man comes towards us. He's well dressed, and as he extends his hand I hear the hint of an accent, like someone who has been living somewhere else for a while. "I flew in from Copenhagen," he tells us. "My name is Scott Willis."

And with that, Lex and I have met the Easter Bunny. And I start to believe in magic again.

EVOLUTION

I turned the group notifications off on the Remembering Judson Memorial Page on Facebook. It only took me a decade.

ESCAPE

I don't mean escapism: going to see a movie on a rainy day or doing drugs to forget your pain. For me, with Tamara, it was about a physical escape: getting out of whatever space she was in. I went to other people's houses after school. I joined clubs and sports teams. I stayed out late, until I knew she would be in bed. I crossed the street when I saw her in the neighborhood in her bright red coat. I slipped outside for a cigarette on Christmas with Judson. And, ultimately, I moved across the country.

Now, at 40, I finally appreciate Toronto: the city, my neighborhood, and, most important, the family home. I'm finally inviting my friends to hang out at the house with me. And I wonder what my life would look like if I hadn't needed to escape so badly.

EPIDEMIC

At first I thought it was just that I was noticing suicide more after Tamara died. The ignorance struck me first: how pervasive it is, how casually one says, "That just makes me want to kill myself" or "Go jump off a bridge."

Then I began to notice the language around the act. What it means to "commit" something. Why that sounds like a crime. The fact that very few people correctly refer to this as a disease.

And as all the language landed around me, I began to see the prevalence of the illness itself. The flurry of suicides in my life that followed Tamara's: three acquaintances in the film industry, a friend's son, random people who were grieving a similar loss smattered across my social network platforms.

Maybe, I thought, *maybe I'm just noticing it more now.*

But also, maybe this is an epidemic.

EVIDENCE

We collect it, as proof. I have been building an arsenal for decades. But the thing about evidence is this: it has to be an outward sign, something plainly visible, and it's never that easy with Tamara. She is not only crazy, she is also crazy smart.

It's nearly impossible (to my mind) to create photographic evidence of lies and deceit. It's impossible to take a photo of the inside of someone's head and to show someone else the whole picture in a single image.

So for years my evidence amounted to only anecdotes. There were always some witnesses, but like most people who witnessed something shocking, it was always indescribable, at least until after the end.

But I presented the evidence regardless of its viability. I thought quantity over quality would surely win out in a case like this. I thought hundreds of anecdotes and missing puzzle pieces and gaps in facts and narratives would be enough.

But it was like screaming into a wind tunnel. My mother didn't want this evidence presented to her. It fell on deaf ears. No one was interested in all the proof I had gathered. Quite the opposite. I was encouraged, often commanded, to "let it go." It wasn't "nice" to call my sister crazy—*just let her be, it's just a little white lie, she just needs attention.*

But it was a LOT of little white lies. A life built of them. Every detail of each imagined and expanded exchange. I worried she wouldn't be able to keep it all straight, that if one card got pulled from the bottom, her whole house would come tumbling down.

Decades. I collected this evidence in my head for decades. And I presented it against my mother's will on a weekly basis.

Then Tamara's psychotic break happened. And then she needed to be institutionalized. And for that we needed a Form 2. And suddenly, all the emails I'd kept and the voicemail messages and the Facebook diatribes and tweets I'd photographed before they were subsequently deleted all had a place—they were needed. Lex and I got to put everything down on paper and attach appendixes and PDF documents and audio files, and it felt like progress. Like all this collecting could amount to something, like saving a life.

But it didn't. It was too little and, to my mind, too late.

Now, after all these decades and with my sister dead in the ground, now my mother wants proof of her own. The first thing she wants is a chronology of events. I'm not sure what "events" she wants listed or who she wants this for.

Lex takes this on, as he always does. The lawyer presents all these details, emotions, near misses, and heart-crushing realities as fact.

> *Mom,*
>
> *As requested, chronology of events is below and copies of all correspondence attached. You'll see that the suicidal thoughts come in bunches. There's a period in mid-October*

(which coincides with when she was doing so well) where
everything seems fine and then it picks back up again in
November, possibly (I would say likely) as the meds wore
off.

April 3, 2016—*Tamara sends an email to Mom re bridges*
and balconies.

September 23—*Tamara sends an email to Mom and Dad*
confessing that she has had suicidal thoughts, following
inquiry from her doctor about it. Detailed description
wondering how people would find out.

September 27—*Tamara emails our stepsister to say she has*
been having suicidal thoughts and ask for advice on
akathisia.

September 30—*Tamara emails Mom and Dad to say she has*
been researching cases of people on Invega committing
suicide.

October 2—*Tamara sends poem to Dad about killing herself*
by jumping off her balcony.

October 4—*Tamara sends a detailed draft of her final sui-*
cide note to a family friend.

October 4—*Tamara sends an email to Mom and Dad com-*
plaining about group therapy.

October 6—*Tamara sends an email to family asking for sup-*
port to overcome suicidal thoughts.

October 6—*Tamara emails Dr. G to say she is contemplating*
suicide.

Mid October: Pax Tamara—*Tamara enjoys a period of tran-*
quility and equilibrium.

October 29—*Email to stepsister re suicidal thoughts*

October 29—*R, our first cousin, comes to Tamara's apart-*
ment; Tamara shows him draft of suicide note.

November 9—Tamara prepares Worksheet as to whether and when she should kill herself; also includes question to self—"Am I serious, or am I just seeking attention."

November 10—Tamara sends email to Allan re being a burden.

November 15—Tamara sends an email to Mom and Dad regarding stopping Invega and suicidal thoughts.

November 15—Tamara sends a Google Chat to Scott Willis saying "T minus 48 hours"

November 17—At 8:29 a.m., Tamara emailed an assistant at Mount Sinai saying she had the flu and would not be attending the group session that day.

November 17—Tamara sent an email to Mom and Dad re money and jobs (3:37 p.m.). No subsequent emails.

November 17—Tamara sets her alarm for 1:30 a.m..

November 18—3:40 a.m.—Death

Lex includes all 18 attachments. And it's enough to get Mom through Christmas. But by January, she is looking for more. By midwinter, every Sunday chat she walks me through an annotated list of Tamara's stuff that she's sorted through in the past week. She says she knows her better now in death than she did in life. She's obsessed.

By spring, the evidence pile is getting slim. Tamara's apartment has been emptied out and is now lived in by some happily oblivious other human. Her childhood bedroom has only stuffed animals and photos and journals left to go through. So my mother reaches further; she has lunch with Tamara's friends, she grills them on whether or not Tamara felt supported by her family, she pulls medical files and psych reports and plows through them one painstaking line at a time.

I don't know what all this evidence is for. It's been seven months since Tamara died, and it doesn't matter anymore. It doesn't matter who was right, how long she was sick, how sick she was, who she told, or who didn't tell us.

It all means nothing, so I ask my mother, "What are you looking for here?"

She tells me, "Just anything that says this isn't my fault."

F

FEAR

We weren't always afraid *of* Tamara. Afraid *for* her?—more often. Afraid for our reputations, our shared group of friends and later, our social networks?—always. But physically, actually afraid of her? That took time.

I was probably the first to be afraid. She was angry at me first. It seemed ridiculous to be afraid of her. It made me feel weak. But she was fierce and furious, and there was always something in her eyes when she was wound up that could make my blood run cold.

And now, as her sickness gets worse and she is home in Toronto, I am hearing stories from my dad about cousins who she approached on the street and made incredibly nervous. And friends are sending me awkward Facebook messages about running into her. And the more often I say, "I hope that was OK," or "You know she's not well," the more I hear the confessional outpouring of their fear when confronted by her. Lex doesn't want his kids to see her alone anymore.

My mother brushes this all away.

Fear can be contagious. But it's more than people starting to catch my feeling. It is that people are actually recognizing that Tamara is dangerous. And it's more than the stories and behaviour now.

It's physical. I can see it. Her eyes roll like she has receded into her head, and what is left out front is empty and disconnected. She has strange shakes, and the skin around her mouth and eyes is dry like she's suffering some kind of dehydration. But the definition of "disease" here is still intangible. If I could point the symptoms out and call it cancer, you would understand. But we don't understand it like that, not yet.

It's December 20, 2015, and my mother has, somewhere in the last few days, experienced a stress fracture of her tibia. It isn't life-threatening, but it's annoying and she's almost 70 and it's exactly what she doesn't need in this moment before Christmas while she's shopping and delivering and decorating and doing in the cold and snow.

Tamara texts me a long and frenetic text about Mom's injury. She is angry and off-kilter and blaming Mom—for what, I have no idea. The text is insane and far too long to want to repurpose here. You'll have to trust me on this. The subject matter ranges from terrorists to love.

In the morning, Mom calls me to tell me that on her way out the door the night before Tamara went on a rant about the Taj Mahal and being spied on and plotted against. Mom said it was really crazy and that Allan had to escort her out of their house. It's the first time I've ever heard a story like this from Mom. She always defends Tamara and can always rationalize her behaviour. Mom goes on to tell me that Tamara is coming to pick her up to go for a coffee and hopefully apologize.

I'm not sure someone who doesn't recognize their own actions can apologize for them. But I don't bother to start this discussion with Mom.

Three hours later, I get another phone call from Mom. She's in tears. She and Tamara went to the Second Cup in Forest Hill Village. Just as they started to sip their cooling coffee, Tamara began to get worked up, so worked up that she started yelling. So my mother gathered her winter coat and her giant purse and her crutches and left to walk the 15 blocks back to the office in the swirling snow. Tamara followed her, trailing behind, at some points yelling and at other moments trying to reconcile. And now Mom is in her office with the door locked behind her, half crying and half laughing into the phone with me. She acknowledges her fear. "I ran away from her," she says to me. "I actually ran away from her."

It's midnight, and Messenger bings with a text from Tamara.

It was actually fun to see Mom. I like being able to look after [her]. When she is on crutches it is the only time she does not run away and we can actually talk and I can do stuff for her. I do love and as always get some small pleasure out of being able to treat and care for someone.

I don't respond. It's midnight, after all.

And now it's four days later, on Christmas Eve, and I am at my brother's house early to help prepare and we are having an actual conversation about where the knives are being locked away.

And now I'm sure we are all afraid.

FUNNY

I'm sure I've figured it out. I'm not guilty. It's funny. It was survival. Right?

Dealing with someone with severe mental health issues is indescribable to those who haven't experienced it. In our family, it was also indescribable to those who refused to acknowledge it or see it. This meant that for years it was just Lex and me. For us it started with shared looks across the table, a knowing glance when the conversation turned or the lie surfaced or the behaviour felt "off." But as Tamara grew increasingly ill, our communication around the issue intensified. We began to talk on the phone on a regular basis, to compare stories, to get updates, to blow off steam, to complain, but mostly to laugh.

We didn't intend for it to be cruel. Quite the opposite. To continue to manage both her illness and my parents' silence, we needed to find a place where this insanity was bearable, and that was in humour. One year, following a Christmas in which Tamara's gift to Lex was a surprise in the trunk of her car (which never materialized) and her gift to me was a nasty letter about what it was like to live with snapping crocodiles, I created a Twitter account just for Lex and me.

The account was called @mayorofcrazy. The mayor only followed other irrational people, including Charlie Sheen, Britney Spears, and an assorted gaggle of other high-profile nut jobs. Then, in 140 characters or less, the account would tweet all the insane things Tamara would say, like, "I am writing a book with the President. It's about cell phone tracking. But I can't tell you about it. I'm being tracked," or "I shaved my head and told my family I was dying of cancer. I told them they would regret it when I was #dead," and even, "Yesterday I told my Dad that my stepfather of 20 years was cheating on my mother. He's not."

While we understood others might find it cruel, it's what we had to do to survive. After all, this came long after the fight with our parents. Long after I yelled and screamed and cried. Years. I had been fighting this for years. I'd first fought my mother (which I'm loath to do), then negotiated with my father, forced family interventions, and lobbied my other siblings. And so I needed to laugh.

I survived by laughing. Sometimes even by ridiculing. I got good at it. Very good. It was quick, and it was relief, not just for me but for my brothers and for Dad. I could even drown out the howling, crazed message that sounded more animal than human that Tamara left on my voicemail with the sound of Lex and me laughing about it.

I pretty much stopped communicating with Tamara directly, yes, but I was still gracious. I was warm at family gatherings and would ask her about life and work, even slid in one-on-one coffee get-togethers, kept the text messages flowing, and eventually returned most of her calls. Even the last texts from me to her are nothing but love.

But I was too wrapped up in the war of my own outrage. I was so angry that no one was listening that I didn't pay enough attention to the small signs.

It's Christmas 2015, and I arrive in Toronto direct from sunny LA just in time to help Mom put a few last decorations on the tree and greet the first snowfall of the season. She tells me that the other kids have all gone home. Lex's daughter was sleepy, and Tamara had caused a scene, and between kids crying and adults yelling, everyone had decided to retire early.

By this point, our Twitter feed is running at full speed, and every detail on Tamara is more than anecdotal. It is fodder! So when my mom tells me that Tamara freaked out because the purple stripe on my brother's shirt identified him as part of the conspiracy and that the Tim Hortons cup on the counter was a message because of how the banana in fruit bowl was pointing at it, my reaction is to take notes. I will definitely need to pull this apart with Lex later.

That humour comes easy to me now. Too easy. It might even be mean. But I add a banana conspiracy tweet to the Twitter feed, get Tamara something generic for Christmas, avoid spending any real time with her, and in my free time with Lex and my friends I am increasingly persistent in finding the funny. It's like a life preserver.

We are all laughing so much that when Tamara gets put in the psych ward for a month and tells everyone there that all her bones have broken and she needs milk to heal them overnight, we don't think it's crazier than anything else we have heard. In fact, as Lex relays these details to me over the phone, I find that they fit the narrative in 140 characters or less.

So on September 17, 2016, two months after Tamara's release and a year since I last updated the Twitter feed, when she texts me to say, *thank you for being there to support Mom over the coming weeks. She will need your caring voice*, I don't notice the complete lack of context.

And when she texts me on September 23, *be good to Mom*, I slam back at her for constantly saying this to me.

I am always good to Mom!

She responds with, *I know. I just want to be sure she can share with someone and she is particularly close to you when it comes to sharing.*

I write back, *absolutely!* just to be done with the conversation.

And on September 29, when I ask how she's doing and she says, *I've been a bit depressed and suicidal*, I roll my eyes and suggest exercise and friends and keeping busy.

The exchange gets so crazy that by the time she gets through some cryptic political stories that reference Guinea and Nicaragua and the downing of the Malaysia Airlines flight and arrives at *lack of a reliable method and concern for Mom are the only two things keeping me alive right now. I need a hug. I sound crazy*, my first thought is, *Yes, yes, you do sound crazy*. And then I laugh at my own joke. I completely miss the message: *lack of a reliable method*.

Now I keep scrolling back in her texts to see if there are any more clues, but when I get to August of 2016, my phone won't scroll back any farther. And I realize I can't take this back. And it's not funny.

FILLER

It's 12 days after my sister's death, and France is driving me to the Whistler Film Festival. I have to moderate a panel and talk in a writer's lab. More than the obligation, it is the need—I need to get away from evidence bags and urns and cemeteries; I need this moment to catch my breath before a long run at home over the Christmas holidays.

It has become habitual—going west to escape Tamara. And this time it is healing. And necessary. But I can't exactly catch my breath. I can't because *everyone knows*. My family spoke publicly about Tamara right away, and Lex's eulogy was posted online and is being shared widely. By the time I arrive at the festival, I am the-girl-whose-sister-jumped.

It's like being the cancer kid. Everyone looks at you with a mix of pity and reassurance.

It's terrible. On the second morning of the festival, I am sitting at a panel when a woman I met only that morning comes and hovers by my seat. She crouches down in front of me and takes my hands in hers and says, "If you ever need someone to talk to . . ."

Are you kidding? I met you over coffee this morning! Are you implying I don't have friends? Of course, I'm only outraged and witty on the inside. On the outside, it's like I've switched off. One sentence in from this woman, and all I can hear is *beeeeeeeeeeeeeeeep*.

My friends swat her away. But no matter how much swatting they do, no one can compete with the deluge of opinions, advice, offers, and anecdotes that flood your life after a crisis. It's about the pile of emails that say, *This happened to my son, my friend, my mother, my daughter* . . . It's about the Facebook posts and messages of love, and the tweets and the texts on mental health. And the people you never heard from before and you've never heard from since. It's the books people want you to read and the tea that they want you to drink, the baths they think you should soak in and the rituals that have worked for them.

And I know there's a lot of kindness in those actions and words, and a lot of good advice between the lines and well-intentioned humans at as much of a loss as I am about how to grapple with the horror of it all.

But it's funny, you know, the stigma of it. Because between all these pitying looks and pious people and emails and posts and books and teacups, there's no space for words like

> *psychotic,*
> or
> *suicide,*
> or
> *epidemic.*

There's no room for how I really feel.

No one wants to hear those words.

Most people are more comfortable with the filler.

FLYING

It is late December 2004.

For the first year in decades, Judson did not ring my doorbell at the family home in Toronto on Christmas Day. He did not deliver my mother a goody basket or sneak me out for a smoke break. He did not return my Boxing Day message. No one is answering the family line at his home.

But I fly back to Vancouver anyway, west and away from him. And then I drive north to the hot springs to celebrate New Year's. I am in a hotel room when my phone rings.

It's Judson.

And he has cancer.

> *He has cancer,* and I am tipping the bus boy.
> *He has cancer,* and I am sipping champagne in a fancy hotel room.
> *He has cancer,* and he is determined to survive it.

I get back to Vancouver a few days later and talk to him again. He has not yet left the hospital. They have kept him. The cancer is called Burkitt's. It is a lymphoma.

It only strikes people under the age of 30. It usually kills people in less than 10 weeks.

But it is not going to kill him—not in the story we tell of our lives. He is big and strong, and they are keeping him to do super doses of chemotherapy immediately. He will get to go home in a few weeks, once they can see how he is taking to the treatment.

I save the number for his hospital room in my phone.

This is when I really become friends with Judson's brother, Josh. I call the hospital room and Judson is getting tested, sleeping, bathing, and Josh brings me up to speed. Half the time Judson is probably there, just lying there, without the energy to talk to anyone, but Josh talks for him. Josh works harder at maintaining the illusion than any of us: the illusion that Judson is fine, that he will survive, that the family is doing OK, that this is process and that it's normal. He crafts this part of the story for most of us, and I think that he is the only one who will ever know the Truth of what happened. Of course, the Truth changes.

It's been less than ten days since I answered my phone in the hot springs hotel. But I know it's time to go home—I can feel it. Home to Toronto, home to my parents, home to see him, sit near him, smell him—home to childhood.

Josh tells me that Judson is having trouble eating and sleeping. A nurse at the hospital had suggested that he smoke a little marijuana to help with these issues. The nurse also said it would take six months to get a medical card so he can get medical marijuana.

And with that I replaced feeling with action. Problem solving. My best space, where I am Teflon. After a few cryptic phone calls, I'm almost packed and ready to fly home.

Security is effortless, but the time standing at the gate makes me anxious about what awaits me on the other end. My heart is beating so loudly on the plane that I am sure the guy next to me can hear it.

I get off the plane and stand at the baggage carousel watching over my shoulder and wondering when the police will approach me. I pick up my bag with everyone else, and no one looks at me funny. Heart still pounding, I walk briskly out of the airport rolling my suitcase behind me and jump immediately into a waiting cab.

———————————

I go to the compassion club, an organization of medical marijuana advocates, buried in Kensington Market. The guy behind the counter provides me with two small jars. One is labelled FEED ME and the other SLEEP ME.

When I get home, I lock myself in the bathroom and pull out the two jars. I feel calm again, and then I feel giddy. Victory! I toss the jars into my knapsack, kiss my mother, and head out the door to trek the familiar path to Judson's house.

It is cold in Toronto, and I am bundled from head to toe as I slip and slide down the Avenue Road hill. I am excited to see Judson. I look forward to giving him a hug and look forward to showing him what I've pulled off and handing over the gifts.

I am not prepared for what he is going to look like.

For how gray his blue eyes have become.

And how hollow his cheeks are.

FRAMED

It's Mother's Day six months after my sister's suicide, and even though the gifts today are meant to all be for Mom, she has come armed with gifts for all of us. We each get a a giant bag, and from those we each pull out two photo frames. They are two feet wide and one foot tall, and each contains a collage of 74 unique photos of Tamara with one image repeated in both frames (a fact my mother is VERY concerned that we know) for a total of 149 images of my sister.

I think, *What the actual fuck? What am I going to do with these?* but instead I say, "Oh, thank you, Mom. This must have been so much work."

I am bewildered. A photograph of your deceased sister among a collection of personal photos in your home or office? Absolutely! An entire shrine of 149 unique photographs dedicated to her . . . I think not.

Mom tells me she is going to ship my copies to my home in Vancouver. We talk about bubble wrap and shipping companies, and after it all I give her a kiss of thanks, and I leave the two giant frames on the kitchen table for shipping. I'm almost out of the room and away from the pictures when she pipes up, "But, sweetie, take these with you! You can keep them in your room for the week that you're here!"

I take the pictures upstairs and leave them outside my bedroom door. When I get home that night, they are in my room, leaning against the fireplace. Somewhere around 3 a.m., I get up and put them facedown in my closet. I leave them there.

The next time I come home to Toronto, the pictures are waiting for me. They have been put back next to the fireplace so that they are the first thing I see. I put them back in the cupboard, but before I leave town two weeks later I take them back out and put them back by the fireplace, for Mom.

Four months later, in Vancouver, I'm racing home to my apartment. I've been away from Toronto a long time, and it's now one day before the death-iversary. I can sense that in the pit of my stomach, but it's not at the front of my mind. Not until I get home, and see that I have a notice of a package from UPS.

And on the day of her death, one year later, I am driving to UPS and picking up the package that contains not one but two very large photo collages of her.

G

GAY

I am not sure when Judson made it official. We had broken up by the time we were 15, sometime during summer camp, but remained fast friends, and he went on to date a couple of other girls, and a couple of boys.

I remember for graduation formal I bought him a pink sequinned shirt from Holt Renfrew that he wore with pride.

GRAVE DIGGER

I've been to more funerals than I am years old. And given more eulogies than most people will in a lifetime. I've lost so many people that I've developed my own lexicon around loss. Words like *death-iversary* and *grief-cation*.

My best friend Paul, who has given me the nickname Death-Pro, swears that there is a business idea in this. "You're a professional at it, Liz."

So it's no surprise to me when the phone rings and it's my mother.

1-800-Death-Pro, how can we help you? I don't actually say this. I say, "Hi, Mom."

"Sweetie, I've thought about it for a while and I've purchased a family plot. Could you come home so we can dig up your sister?"

I was four years old when the quadruplets were born and my infant sister Katherine died—or maybe she was murdered. A nurse at the hospital was suspected of killing babies—forty-three died in the cardiac unit the year that Katherine died, a spike of over 600 percent—and there was a big court case, although the nurse who was charged with murder was eventually acquitted. I was young so I didn't understand what was going on, and yet I did. It was my first loss and it was fundamental and as a result, I'm the child who doesn't even question it.

"I'd be happy to fly home and dig up some bodies with you, Mom," I say. I wanted to go for reasons that I can't even begin to really explain to the average Muggle. But it was too close to the start of my next project, and too expensive to fly, and too much . . . so instead I call her the next day.

She needs to talk, I can tell. And it's about Great-Aunt Tillie. Aunt Tillie pretty much outlived everyone who might have loved her. So by the time she died, the only relative left in spitting distance of the Toronto funeral home was my mother. So the urn came to our house. For the past 15 years, Great-Aunt Tillie has been "living" in our basement next to the freezer, her closest neighbor the frozen lasagna.

"I think we should bury Tillie when we bury your sister, if there's room," she says.

And this statement from her prompts a trip to the cemetery later, when I am in town, to check out the aforementioned, recently purchased family plot. There *is* room for Tillie, but Mom wants to overanalyze it anyway. She even has diagrams. If she had her way, she would draw her own chalk outline just to make sure that everyone fits.

We finally climb back in the car and my mother starts the engine but doesn't drive anywhere.

"Unless you get cremated, there won't be space for you . . ." she says.

I'm OK with that.

When it's finally time to go to the cemetery to dig up Katherine, Tamara is the only child available and willing to do this with Mom. Tamara was always willing to take care of my mother. Tamara and Mom bundle Great-Aunt Tillie in her urn into the car. Mom tries to put Tillie in the trunk, but Tamara insists on the back seat. "She'll want to look out the window. I think she'll like that." So the three of them pile into the car and spend the ride to the cemetery pointing out to Tillie all the things that have changed in the city since she has been in the basement. As Mom tells me this story, I'm giggling so hard I nearly manage to forget how morbid it all is.

They arrive at the cemetery and go to the graveside, where they're met by a large, bearded grave digger. According to Tamara, he grunted an acknowledgment but didn't seem to speak much. Not even to the guys who get shovels out of the truck and pry the stone from Katherine's grave.

Tamara tells me that she tried to make Mom laugh or distract her. "Look, Mom," she said. "Great-Aunt Tillie is waiting patiently for us." But Mom is not laughing. Just a feeble smile and she brushes the dirt away from Katherine's name and attempts to clean off the edges of the stone. It makes sense to me. They are digging up her daughter, after all.

Time crawled. Apparently, there was a lot of digging. And digging. First to make the hole deep, and then to make it wide. I remember reading somewhere that the soil has a tendency to shift below the surface so urns and even coffins can move up to a foot or more from their original resting place.

By the time the grave digger gets out the metal detector, my mother is in tears. Tamara is finding it hard to keep her engaged. And Mom can't take it anymore.

She approaches the grave digger, reaches out to clutch his forearm, and, crying, asks, "Does this happen often?"

He is painstakingly slow with his response. "No, ma'am, the bodies usually go the other way."

GOODBYE

I try to kill time, to erase it, to stop counting down or up or away from the moments I have here, now. Branded with the cancer band on my arm, I spend those weeks in Toronto wandering aimlessly. I wander hospital corridors, city streets, and then, to escape the biting February winds, down into the malls that lie beneath the city. I've been wandering there for weeks. Toronto is built that way. You can do that.

And it feels like I'm underground, or underwater. There's no natural light in this life right now, and people are always crying around me. The smell of the hospital has become too familiar. I'm sick of the waiting room. Even Judson's house with all the whispering and the tiptoeing is getting to me. I'm sick of getting hit by the waves of other people's emotions.

While he is in the hospital, I squeeze in meetings and lunches and drinks with other people. I laugh with my friends—*our* friends, even! I go to parties and have dinners with my family. I even take the time to reach out to people I haven't seen or spoken to in months.

Judson goes up to his family cottage for a few days in the middle of my stay. I have the gall to be angry with him. How is it possible that I waste a day, an hour, or even a second of my last moments on earth with him?

All my insecurities come to the surface when he is away: maybe he doesn't like me anymore; maybe we've grown apart. I race through the rationalizations. I've come home, I've supported, I've smuggled puppies into hospital rooms, and I'm running out of solutions. Now work is calling. Someone else needs me, and I need to function. My flight is booked. And it's a relief.

Then I remember, he is dying, he has cancer, and I am, clearly, an asshole.

We crawl out through his window on my last day in town. The way we always used to. We sit on the roof and smoke a joint. He talks about Josh. How worried he is about him. I get high. And listen. Just to the sound of his voice more than the words that he says.

If I don't leave for the airport soon, I will miss my flight. At the door I give Judson a hug, and Kathy's eyes meet mine over his shoulder. I know that she is telling me, *This is the last time you will see him.* I hold on tighter, as tight as I can, but just for a moment. I don't want him to know how sad I am. And Kathy looks so sad as she watches us that I have to fight back my own tears.

As we part, I look him in the eye. I look as hard and as deep as I could. For a minute we click in—back to that place where we could stare at each other for hours. A gaze. Love.

I turn, walk down the stairs and almost make it to the end of the driveway before the tears come. I spend the entire walk home memorizing him: the look on his face, his eyes, and his heart.

I feel anxious going to the airport and claustrophobic boarding the airplane. But then I land at home, and it is easier to forget all about the anxiety, the trip, the creepy hospital with its funny smell and the crying family members in the waiting room. I forget about the plastic box that he had inserted into his chest so the chemo meds could be injected into him, and the chunks of hair missing from his head.

It feels like months since he first called me in my hotel room to tell me he was sick. What is two more weeks? At least, that's what I tell myself.

GOOGLE

It's been 11 months since she died, and I just googled her for the first time.

The first article is her obituary. It's not even her obituary, actually—it's just the small piece we released announcing her death (Is that right? Announcing?). It's posted on a link to the funeral home. The third article is the same announcement that was printed in *The Globe and Mail*. Between them both is a link to an article in *The Globe and Mail* from March 2003 about my father and his work, entitled "Mr. Conflict of Interest." Then there are the usual links to her Facebook, Twitter, and LinkedIn profiles, and as you move to the second search page, the stories of her start to filter out and other Tamara Levines begin to take her place.

The first four photos on the image search are of her. So is the seventh photo.

And I think, *That's it. That's all there is.* But as I scroll to the bottom of the Google page, there is a section that reads, "searches related to Tamara Levine," and this is what that gives me:

Levine quadruplet endowment
Tamara Levine death
Katherine Levine obituary

Levine quadruplets Toronto
Tamara Ashley Levine Toronto
Tamara Levine obituary
Michael Levine daughter
Carol Cowan Levine

I'm struck by the size and scope of the tragedy here.

HARD DRIVE

It's been five or six days since she died, and Mom is taking me to her apartment "to see." And I want to know what needs to be done and how much there is to do and how I can help. I don't yet know that Mom will spend years of her life sorting through Tamara's things or that every trip home to Toronto will involve another layer of unravelling. I'm just looking to go one step at a time, to follow Mom's lead. I want to know what I can accomplish in these first eight days at home.

And so we start with her apartment. Or it seems like we might, except . . . As Mom starts talking and pointing and suggesting what might move I follow her lead, but every time I touch something Mom tells me to put it down or says, "That can wait." It's clear I can't do anything, so I sit down on Tamara's couch and just watch and listen to her.

When we find Tamara's camera, I instantly know that it's the only thing of hers I want to keep. I don't understand yet how holding it in my hands and feeling the click of the shutter will prove meditative and soothing for me. I don't know yet that Tamara foresaw this and left me a letter in the bottom of the case. I don't know that the letter acknowledges that she bought this camera because I wanted the same model. I don't know anything but my instinct in this moment—that this is supposed to come home with me.

Now Mom is into the tech equipment, and she is starting to find a place for me to support her. "What's this?" she asks repeatedly as she pulls cables and Kobos and iPods and Blackberrys from Tamara's office space.

And I see the space in which I can help. "Let me take all this, Mom," I say. She hesitates, but I already know what she wants. "I'll take every photo and every piece of writing and everything you could want from all these devices and put it on a hard drive and have it for you by Christmas. Then you'll have everything in one place and you can just plug it into your computer whenever you want to."

It seems easy enough. I am relatively tech savvy, and Tamara left us passwords for everything along with her suicide note, and I figure I'll just compile all the files and do a drag and drop and that will be that.

Once I get home to Vancouver, I start with her Blackberry. It's the usual jumble of text messages and emails and random photos. Only two things stand out here: The first is a text to Scott Willis that says only *T-minus 48 hrs* that she sent exactly 48 hours before her death. The second is that she has kept screenshots of the last few times I called her . . . like she wanted a record of the fact that I had tried, that I liked her, that she mattered to me somehow.

I am shaken, but it isn't that bad really. It's almost done. And finally, on Christmas Eve, I figure I'll tackle her computer so Mom has the drive in her hand as promised. The first thing I find on Tamara's computer breaks my heart. It's just a Word document, but . . . it's all her heart, all her pain, and all her crazy.

It reads like this:

I stood in the hot tub for 15 minutes trying to remember when I last felt happy or free . . .

I tried as hard as I could to remember a moment when I was happy to see someone . . .

When a conversation or action did not feel pre-scripted, probing, a blatant violation of privacy and lacking all authenticity.

I tried to remember when last someone picked up the phone to call me or even sent me an email without a pre-scripted message with intentional typos or coincidental names of some variety.

I tried to remember what it was like to swim or work out without cameras watching or people watching from above in purple or testing in some way.

I tried to remember what it was like to run into a friend without them running away in fear of being investigated, coerced or mowed down by the US, 5i, Russian, Iranian, Israeli mafia or some other variety of illusionary shark.

I tried to remember what it was like to be trusted and to trust in return.

I consider whether it's OK for Mom to read this. And I realize that it's not my call to make. It may be painful and revealing, and part of me wants to protect Tamara, but there is nothing nefarious here—and I can't keep this from my mother.

I keep trudging through—academic papers, bits of research, some creative musings, and then photos. They are tough to look at, but most of them are good, and I know Mom will want to keep these. I delete a couple that are inappropriate or private, but I have no guilt about these removals—I'm protecting Tamara's privacy, after all.

Her drive is almost empty now, save for a file with videos. A bunch of the videos are academic content from research presentations or proposals. I find a couple of really sweet videos of her laughing on the living room floor with my little brother, Joshy. The videos make me smile a little bit, and they make me cry. And then there is one video left, and I am so close to being through this painfully intimate place, and I'm relieved. Then I see the date—the video was taken on the day she died, just over a month ago, and it is ten seconds long . . .

I watch it. Twice. And remove it.

I am the only one who has ever seen it.

And the only one who ever will.

HELP

There isn't any. No one is going to make this better. Nothing is going to make this better.

HELPFUL

The first night of shiva for Judson is madness. By the time we get to the house from the cemetery, there is already a crowd gathering. Coats litter the front hallway area, and Josh and I are hurled into function mode. Neither of us complains. This is what we want to be doing. We are happy to organize. Refill ice. Pour drinks. Replace plates of canapés. We do not want to have awkward conversations with the adults; we do not want to talk about Judson, or our feelings. We certainly don't want to hear any more about anyone else's feelings.

Our friends look uncomfortable already, and we've only been here half an hour. They don't know the house well enough to make themselves busy, to escape the endless conversations, or to not notice the cloth draped over all the mirrors, the hushed sobs from the corners of the room, or the pain in Kathy's eyes. Judson's friend Tyler and I connect across the room. He wants the young people to get out of here, to go to his house, to celebrate a life instead of to mourn it. And then Kathy needs me. Or at least she needs someone, and I need to function. We're the perfect match.

The extra drinks are downstairs in the fridge next to Judson's bedroom. I haven't been downstairs yet, since he died. I stand at the freezer door staring aimlessly at the myriad beverages, and I see someone slip into his room.

His room! As if his privacy no longer mattered, as if it was not his anymore.

No one should go in there. That is his space, our space. I don't even know the person who just slipped in, then out, and shut the door behind him. I go find Josh. Tug on his arm and point towards Judson's room to say, *I'm going there.* I go, close the door behind me, and wait for Josh to follow.

I am frozen in his space. Bed still creased from his last sleep at home, magazines left open and desk piled high with cards and sunglasses and scraps of paper—like he'll be back any minute now. I am paralyzed. Stuck in a time warp, waiting to hear his voice, for his door to open, for this moment to end in any way except the inevitable. I lie on his bed, just breathing him in. Have I been here for seconds, minutes, more—waffling between the fictional hope and the reality of the despair?

And then Josh is there. Function mode.

We open drawers and cupboards and rummage through them. In the bedside table: condoms, cock rings, porn magazines, lube, it all gets thrown into my knapsack. In the bottom bedside table drawer, two jars, still half-full that read SLEEP ME and FEED ME. And beside them, another ziplock bag packed with marijuana.

Josh works on Judson's desk, and from there we get a journal, some pills that look like ecstasy, a container of GHB, and cocaine: small bags of cocaine and a small glass cocaine dispenser that's almost full. Josh looks to the sky. "This is the last time we're bailing you out, buddy," he says. We lock the door, and Josh taps out a small line for each of us on the desk. Lines done, Josh slips back to check on his mum, leaving me with instructions to finish by going through the closet.

On the floor of the closet is a shoebox. I don't even realize what it is until I am halfway through the first piece of paper. Then it dawns on me. He kept my letters, all of them. Most still had the original envelopes. I watch the blue ink of his address bleed into the paper, and I wipe away the tears smudging the page. The letters go into the knapsack. They are mine, after all.

And then I feel sick. I don't know if it is the drugs or just being in his space, but I have to get out of here. I rummage through the box and find a few more baggies with powder at the bottom. They go into my knapsack with everything else, and I am out the door to the shiva before I can look at his space again. I leave before I can curl up on the creases that he left on his bed and never get up again.

Keep moving. Stay helpful. I learned this young. It means that I don't have to feel.

Josh and I finally leave and go to Tyler's. It is quiet when we get there, but there is a pile of shoes in the front hall that suggests a serious party.

Upstairs, everyone is sitting silent, sipping beer, crying, hugging, not "celebrating" his life at all. I wander through the living room into the middle of the crowd.

"Judson couldn't make it tonight, but he sent you this."

And with that, I slide my knapsack off my shoulders and empty the entire contents onto the coffee table.

I get a few laughs.

Emboldened, someone across the room grabs a baggie and puts a line of cocaine on the mantelpiece. An honourary line, for Judson. Someone else prints out his picture and tapes it up.

Soon a joint and a glass of champagne have been set up beneath the picture, too.

It turns into a party.

We get high, we laugh, and we cry. We play our music too loud. People come and go, but the three of us, Tyler, Josh, and I, are constants. We don't sleep for five days.

I walk home with my headphones playing in my ears and a baggie of blow in my pocket. It is a long walk, but I barely notice a single step. I do a couple of keys when I feel tired or sad, and I turn my music up. By the time I get to my street, streaks of light are bleeding into the night sky, my nose is bleeding into a worn Kleenex, and my head is pounding.

Sleep.

I wake up the day after our five-day shiva ends; it might be two days after. I stand under the hot shower for what seems like forever. The house is empty. My mother left me a note on the front hall table— hoping I was feeling "better."

Fuck. I am not feeling "better." I am feeling worse. We have prayed and sung and buried and ritualized and drunk and laughed and cried, and then it ended. And I woke up this morning and everything is still so fucking wrong.

The end is devastating. The end makes me understand. Commitment to not feeling this is a lifetime promise.

HIGH SCHOOL

I really miss him. Often, and still, a dozen years later.

I don't really miss her.

She has not been a part of my daily life for decades. While I note her absence at family affairs, it is more with a sigh of relief than a twinge of loss—because these moments are easier without her.

I have some semblance of control over my emotions. I always have. And while I grieve Tamara at moments, I have not yet been really sideswiped by this loss. I held my own at the funeral, the gathering, out in public, and then even back at home. I now cry when I need to, and beyond that, my life without her is not so much different from my life with her—in either case, she isn't a part of it.

So I'm more shocked than anyone when grief takes me out at the knees.

I'm back in Toronto for some meetings and some work. I don't notice her absence here anymore. She hadn't lived at home for years, so Mom's place is becoming a newfound sanctuary of sorts, and I don't venture upstairs to her childhood bedroom often, if ever.

While I'm in the city this week, my high school is giving out Distinguished Old Girl Awards. My friend Larysa is a recipient this year, so five of us are going to go, all together. We've known one another for decades. Each one of them was present with me when Judson died and again the week of Tamara's funeral. Within minutes of my arrival at the school, my friends show up, and it's laughs and hugs and VIP receptions and familiar and familial. Now I'm certain this is going to be easy. I've known some of these women for over thirty years. I am safe here.

As we wander down the hall to the reunion dinner, I can hear my friends' voices behind me and in front of me, and I'm not engaged in any conversation, but in the normalcy of it all: how they speak, the sound of their laughter. I love these people. These people, I miss.

The dinner is in the gymnasium. A place familiar to me but different tonight, filled with tables and chairs and a stage. We raise a glass to Larysa—she makes a lovely speech. And we mill about for a bit drinking wine. There are a few tables off to our left that are celebrating their twenty-year reunion. It takes me a moment to realize that it's Tamara's grad class. There are so many of them. They all seem to want to talk to me, I can feel it. But none of them do.

As the dinner ends, we decide to walk through the school with the last of our wine and go back to the chapel, where we had assembly every morning. It seems simple enough. But as we meander down the long corridor to the old section of the building, I can feel my discomfort growing. When my friends stop to hover in front of grad photos posted on the wall, I push to move on. I can feel Tamara staring out at me.

At the end of the hall is the small math classroom where the folk group used to rehearse at lunch hours. A room where I spent hundreds of hours and a room where, once I graduated, Tamara, in her compulsive need to copy me, did the same.

And for the first time in a year and a half, out of nowhere, I feel her. I see her here, in her school uniform, tie askew, knapsack too big for her and sliding off one shoulder. I hear her voice and her laugh. There's a sudden, overwhelming awareness of the size of the hole she has left, and I could fit this entire school into it.

I didn't stop to consider that I haven't been back to the school since. That it was the only space I shared with her. That this might be hard.

None of it.

There are tears in my eyes, rolling down my cheeks, and I can't breathe. Only my oldest friend, Robin, notices, so we hang back from the group to let the moment pass.

I wipe my eyes and giggle. It's something I do to ease the pressure. Apparently, I do it on film sets, too. Robin looks worried, but I shrug it off and we continue down the hall to the chapel. I can make the tears stop for a minute, but that's just long enough to free Robin from this burden. I can't pull myself together, maybe for the first time ever, so I just sit there in the dark and cry and listen to the sounds of my friends' laughter like they are on the other side of the ocean, and I hope their voices are enough to carry me through this and across to the other side.

I don't know how long I'm here. Robin is now reenacting her role as the angel Gabriel in the Christmas nativity to shrieks of giggles. As I sit and watch, I remember the night we performed the nativity, the night that Natalie's Mom died. Natalie had to go the hospital and Robin went with her, leaving instructions for us to meet them there.

She was dressed in her Angel Gabriel costume, and she walked Natalie down the corridor with the stern headmistress, who said to them, "It's not often that you have an actual angel with you in moments like this."

Robin *is* an angel. And something I've noticed about loss is its direct correlation to gratitude. I wipe my tears, and give thanks for my friends. They are angels. And I'm going to be OK.

INTERVAL

I've had a good run. No one has died in the last few years.

IMAGINED

I used to imagine what those last three months were like for Judson. I would lie awake and wonder about his fear, about the things he missed, about the details he kept in his head or those that only Josh heard through Judson's drugged and fevered bouts of chemo.

Later, I wondered if I'd still like Judson today. I wondered if we would have grown in the same direction and stayed as close as we were or if it's possible that we might have grown apart. That I wouldn't like him now.

But always and most often, I wondered if he was afraid. Afraid of fighting, of losing, of dying, of death, of pain.

I wondered my way through the details. Did he think about his new mortgage, law school applications, the new boy was flirting with? We never really talked about those things after his diagnosis.

Was he annoyed when he first got sick or was he worried? Was he frustrated with how long he had to wait in the emergency room? Did he care that he had plans: Christmas with me, Jewbouree, a trip to the cabin up north? Was he restless, or had he somehow already let life go?

I wonder how he felt when they told him he had cancer. What was it like to hear the C word? Did it flatten him, or was his instantaneous response the same one he had for us days later: that he was way too young and too beautiful to die? Did fear feel contagious when he had to tell people about it, to say the details out loud, the scary names and the big words? I wonder how it felt to hear all of us hear his news.

I spent hours in my head trying to understand what it was like for an athlete like him to lose his body: to constantly be sick to his stomach, to need help going to the bathroom, to have people poke and prod and talk about him? I wonder what it was like to lose his muscle, his physical power, his privacy, his dignity, his independence.

I wonder if he ever gave up and how he struggled with that. Did it ever feel like there were two of him: one that knew he was dying and one that refused to believe it? I wonder if dying feels easier in those moments. Like giving in.

I can't know the answers to any of these questions. And the only answer I didn't want to know I got: that as they wheeled him to the ICU with Josh holding his hand, his last words were, "I'm so scared."

Thankfully, Josh lied to him. The way we all would. He told him it would be OK.

INTERVENTION

Christmas holidays of 2012: I put in my final and biggest fight for Tamara. I force a family intervention, replete with competent shrink at a professional office and Mom and Dad and all of us in the same room for the first time in years. That night, a lot of people spoke, but I mostly stayed quiet. I had only one thing to say: "I think you're very sick. And I want you to get better."

It didn't work. Tamara denied everything and left that night adamant that Hillary Clinton was checking her emails, that everyone should stop communicating with her that way for our own protection, and that we would see, we were all wrong about everything.

Nonetheless, we sent this email from my account:

> *To: Tamara*
> *CC: Lex and Pete*
> *Date: December 19, 2012*
>
> *Dear Tamara,*
>   *Thank you so much for having the courage to come and talk with us last night. It meant a lot and is a great step forward.*

With the holiday events ahead all three of us just wanted to take a moment to address how we keep these times positive and fun—they are not times to work out all of our issues. All of the disagreements and details will be addressed over time with a professional helping us. But, for our holiday time together and for our parents we need to focus on the good stuff, the positives and remember how much fun we can have together.

Looking forward to it.

Warmest,
Liz, Pete, Alexis

And she sent this as a response:

To: Liz, Peter, Alexis, Michael, and Carol
Liz. Please do not email as requested. Thank you. Tamara

This is where we always got to. That place where the only thing we could do was laugh. She was stuck in her constructed narrative about global conspiracy theories and emails being tracked. And Lex knew I'd be hurt and frustrated, so he was quick to spin it back to Peter and me.

To: Liz, Pete, Dad [he often left Mom out of these as she didn't find solace in the humour—it hurt her]

Dear Hillary Clinton,
If you are reading this email, please know, we think you are doing great work.
Except for the whole thing with the espionage and the little underage children. Tamara told us all about it. Sounds like an unfortunate business.

Anyway, say hi to Bill.

The Levine Clan
Lex

It made me laugh. I could count on Lex for that. And so we let it settle. But Christmas with her was a shit show. So after Christmas we sent this.

To: Tamara
Date: December 26, 2012

Tamara,

We are very grateful that you made an effort to come together with the family again this holiday, and to make two holiday dinners (Chanukah and Christmas Day) peaceful and serene. Thank you for that. Thank you also for your generous Christmas gifts.

We appreciate the strong and painful emotions you go through with family. That said, we are quite troubled about [your] behaviour . . .

. . . We are speaking with a single voice and asking you to accept the help being offered. We've found the professional—who seems excellent—and we're all willing to make the time to be there. The cost is covered. It is long past time that these inappropriate behaviours—which by your own admission arise when you are uncomfortable—are resolved.

We all really do love that good, sweet, generous Tamara—our sister, our family, and our friend. We wouldn't be going to this trouble if that were not true.

It is also true, however, that we are exhausted by

*three decades of boundary-crossing, attacks and manip-
ulation. I can only imagine you are exhausted, too. Surely
you want, and have expressed a desire for, a more loving,
peaceful existence.*

*Please come on January 7th to continue the process
and journey towards well-being and health. If you choose
not to, if you honestly believe that you do not need to
change and grow—and that everyone else does (and you
will only accept help when others do), then you will be
very disappointed by the consequences. Those being ex-
tremely narrow and limited family relationships—if any at
all, rather than the healing, loving family we all hope for.*

Alexis, Pete, and Liz

January 7th came and went, and the appointment was cancelled,
and I might have lost all hope except that now that the intervention
had happened it felt like I had allies.

My father acknowledged the full breadth of her illness, and for the
first time Peter was really on side and understood that she wasn't
well. Lex was more proactive than he had ever been, and even my
mother could no longer completely deny what I was seeing.

So I took a break from the battle. People knew. It wasn't just me
anymore. I could let go.

And I did.

That was when my relationship with Tamara really ended. I don't
think I talked about her for an entire year.

INSTINCT

I am not a religious person. I think motivational quotes are bullshit. I do not believe in self-help books, and no amount of wishing or even believing is going to bring you a Lamborghini or a cure for cancer. Despite my cynicism, I believe wholeheartedly in feelings, in connections to people and moments. I believe these relationships have the ability to collapse the boundaries of time and space.

I was connected to Judson.

"Connected" is one of those words whose definition sits just beyond our reach, and although the origin of the adjective is a place I have rarely visited, it seems somehow unwittingly selfish not to attempt it.

When I wake up on the day he is going to die, Vancouver is sunny and warm and it should be raining. I am on the road early and going to make it to work with time to spare. Despite being ahead of the clock, I have the sense I am late for something from the moment I wake up.

I pull into my parking spot with my heart pounding, the blood rushing in my ears.

And then I know.

Connected: to me, to my heart.

I am running to a studio a block away, and I think I left the door of my car unlocked, but it doesn't matter. The elevator is too slow, so I take the six flights of stairs two at a time. I am still running when I hit the office door and pick up the phone to call the hospital. I finish dialing and can hear nothing but my heart pounding, and I think it might beat right out of my chest.

For the first time in weeks, neither Judson nor Josh answer the phone in his room. A nurse picks up the phone, and I stumble through my request to talk to Judson. Her voice is gentle, apologetic, and I am instantly angry. The stumble is gone. The anger hurls me into action. *Get me to him. Transfer me. Now.*

The call is transferred.

I fight to keep my voice even as I ask for him again. An RN in ICU makes a call on the other line. I wait on hold, biting back the urge to scream. A nurse transfers me again, "upstairs" this time. For the third time I ask to speak to Judson; it will be the last time I ask for him and expect an answer. They tell me they can only take calls from family. Fighting back the hysteria, I tell them I am family. I ask for Kathy.

Her voice on the line is numb, absent: "We just lost him five minutes ago."

Five minutes ago. What was I doing five minutes ago? What about ten? What if I had gone back to Toronto on the flight yesterday instead of planning to leave tomorrow? What if they were wrong? What about the plan we had to watch WWF that night with Josh—he had made the plans, and he always stuck to his plan.

Somewhere during those thoughts Kathy passes the phone to Josh. Josh sounds deadpan, like he is in shock. And I know we both need to do something. Anything. Anything that feels like helping Judson, or saving him, or bringing him back.

And there it is. The plan. A plan. The place where I am safe. Josh and I immediately make a list of friends we need to call and then break the list of phone calls in half. I have almost 30 calls to make. If I start right away, I can get through half of them before I have to be on set.

I leave it at that. I hang up, and I sit and stare at the phone for maybe a minute. I can hear the seconds ticking away on the office clock. It is quiet because I can't talk yet. I'm not ready to say this out loud. I know that it will make it true. A new story.

The first call is the hardest. Karina makes every other call seem simple. She breaks. There is no other way to describe the wail that I hear, the clatter of her phone on her desk, the sound of her coworkers rushing to check on her, to hold her up. A nice woman comes on the phone and tells me that she is so sorry for my loss and that they will take care of Karina, that she will call me back when she can.

With every call, I have to listen to the loss land on someone new. The range of emotion is overwhelming, from hysteria and tears to anger and absolute silence. I even have a couple of people who giggle nervously. I think around the ninth call I turn my response system off. Shut down.

Only 40 minutes until my call time. I'm like a machine. Six more calls and I'm back to work.

Teflon.

J

JUDSON

He was always tall. Even when he wasn't, he was: long and lanky and constantly tripping over his two left feet. It was only in the water that it all came together—he swam, and he rowed. It was always surprising to me that he travelled in such straight lines this way. Water was the only place that he did.

JOSH

Today someone asked me if I think Tamara stole a life that some-one like Judson was meant to have.

What?

NO!

I never thought that for a second.

People ask me if I'm angry at Tamara.

I'm not.

Don't get me wrong, I was. For years. But once other people began to understand how sick she was, once everything became insanity, once she was in the hospital, how could I be angry? By then my anger had plenty of places to land: my parents, the hospital, the system—but none of it landed on Tamara.

In losing themselves, both Tamara and Judson had a way of being selfless. In the last months of her life, Tamara texted me over and over again to "take care of Mom." In the last weeks of his life, Judson asked me to look out for his little brother, Josh. "Just don't let him get lost," he said.

I have done everything in my power to take care of my mother, from holding her hand to traipsing the cemetery measuring out family plots, because, quite simply, it's what you do. I could fulfill that obligation. With Josh it was different.

Josh had a tough go of life in the years before Judson got sick. He lost a baseball scholarship, got too into drugs, and then got crushed by the model he was dating, who was too young to handle Judson's death (weren't we all?) and in doing her best might have broken his heart. The poor boy was just generally a little lost.

Judson was a much more patient older sibling than I was. Judson wanted to make sure that Josh would be OK. He wanted me to look out for him.

"You know . . . in case," he said.

"Happy to help, but he's got you. He only wants to hear that stuff from you. You'll be back on your feet soon."

"I need you to promise," he said, looking at me with his once-blue eyes. I could see the panic and the pain behind them.

"I promise."

I meant it when I said it. My present self, standing in front of him, meant every bit of it. You can't look into the eyes of a dying friend and not mean it. But I could feel the impossibility of it. Even as I was saying it.

I spent a lot of time with Josh around Judson's illness and death. To me, it feels like I shared this experience with him and him alone. An intimate, silent, gut-wrenching sharing. Everything between us was soaked in Judson. It still is.

After the funeral, I stuck around Toronto for a bit. My family was used to having me live away, and so didn't expect me to do anything, and Josh's family was walking like zombies through their own routines. So we were completely without obligations, beyond those we had to each other. Who would expect the brother and best friend of a dead twentysomething to be functional? Everyone just gave us time and space, maybe too much of both . . .

So we got high. We went for walks across the city that would take hours. We would set up base camp in bars from 2 p.m. until 2 a.m. We would drop by Josh's house at 2 or 3 a.m. to pick up some snacks or drinks or to crash on the couch for a couple of hours and watch *South Park*. No matter what time we stopped at his home, Kathy was sitting at the dinner table doing sudoku, the house dark and only the dining room table light dimmed above her head.

I tried not to let this get to me: how sad Kathy looked sitting there, and how small. How much cocaine we were doing, how badly I was breaking my promise to Judson.

But still that promise stayed with me, always. As I flew back to Vancouver and stepped back into my life, I did keep up with Josh. I texted him. I visited when I was in Toronto. I pushed him to see me, to come out, to speak, to talk about Judson.

At one point we had a conversation about how hard it was to see each other, how much Judson was present in every exchange between us. And so we took a break for a little while.

But even that year we exchanged texts on Jusdon's death-iversary.

LIZ
Sending you love today

JOSH
Thanks. Always needed on this day

And then Tamara died.

Josh promised he would come to the funeral. Or at least for drinks after. He didn't do either. Later that week, he admitted to me that it was all too much. And I understood.

Because I do understand now: I remember how much Judson defined his life, and I know hard this all is. I get why he was drinking so much, why he is slow to respond and often a no-show, and why Karina and Kathy are always on about him. I also understand that he's surfacing. I can see how close he is to winning this battle. And maybe, just maybe, I am starting to understand how I can help him. I have learned to listen, to accept him for who and how he is now.

Through him, I have learned, finally, not to judge.

Somehow, I am finding the patience and love to do for him what I could never do for her.

JOKES?

Death can bring out the best in people. It can also bring out the worst.

As my father stood in his kitchen that morning with tears rolling down his face, it brought out the worst. The first thing my stepmother, Donna, said to him was, "I can't believe she didn't copy me on the suicide note."

And I wish that were the worst of her moments . . .

The evening before the funeral, Mom has everyone over to the house for dinner, and she includes Donna, of course. As we sit down together, Mom begins to explain the layout of the funeral home—seven seats in the front row on each side of the aisle—and she wants the blood family to sit together. She suggests that everyone's partners can sit in the row behind. This will allow them to console and support and be in touching distance, but it will also allow Mom and Dad to grieve for their daughter together and to be surrounded by their surviving children. Everyone agrees this is a good idea.

Well, almost everyone.

As Dad and Donna get into the car to go home, sleep, and prepare for the funeral, Dad thanks her for being present and supporting my mother's decisions. She slips into the front seat of his BMW to head home to their mansion and manages only, "The second row? I feel like Rosa Parks."

JUMP

It has been 11 months. Lex just posted a suicide awareness ad on his Facebook wall. It features a young guy who jumped off the Golden Gate Bridge. One of the very few survivors. It's a good ad, I guess. It says all the right things and ends with encouragement to reach out for help.

But it's a miss for me.

Tamara reached out for help. In retrospect, she reached out for help everywhere. She showed our first cousin R her suicide note in October, she messaged and texted all of us, and a month before she died, she posted publicly on Facebook, writing, *I had a mental and physical breakdown on July 31st that resulted in a month in hospital and diagnosis with a delusional disorder. By sharing this so publicly I am trying to reduce the stigma and isolation . . . Despite amazing support from friends and family I have felt really isolated and alone and at times suicidal.*

But the problem is that when everything that comes out of someone's mouth is incoherent and a plea for attention, by 20 years later, you stop listening. Maybe these ads should teach us how to listen instead of encouraging us all to speak . . .

So I'm learning to listen in a new way. I'm trying to hear Lex: Why did he post this? And I'm trying to hear myself: Why can't I shake it? And what I hear, when I listen, are the details.

It's about how he (the subject of the video) felt that everyone around him was out to get him, trying to hurt him, and trying to kill him. And about how Tamara had those delusions too.

It's about how he vividly remembers writing his suicide note. And about the 11,000-word letter she left for all of us.

It's about the 25 stories of his fall. And the 29 stories of hers.

It's about how the minute his hands left the railing, he instantly regretted his decision.

I think about Tamara, and how much we, the survivors, regret ours.

K

KNOWN

The last I spent any real time with Tamara was in March of 2016, almost eight months prior to her death.

I am in the middle of shooting a VW commercial when she comes to Vancouver. I don't really have time to answer her calls, or anyone's, but I have sent her a text and we have made a plan for her last day in town.

March 5, 4:42 a.m., she leaves me a message, and the vibrating of the phone reaches into my sleep. I have been home and in bed for less than two hours. I don't listen to the message until I wake up in the morning.

And when I do, it makes my blood run cold. It sounds more animal than human. She's sobbing, howling into the phone and crying my name over and over again.

I call her en route to the Airbnb she is staying at. I ask her about the voicemail message. She says she just had cramps and was calling to whine about them.

I know that's nowhere close to the truth.

I pick her up and get her luggage into the trunk and take her to the Alibi Room for breakfast. The conversation is normal in parts and crazy in others. She excuses herself to go to the bathroom at some point. She's gone a long time. Long enough for me to check my email and send a couple of texts. Long enough for me to notice. When she comes back, she asks me if the lights in that washroom tell me when to turn my head to the right or the left.

I am worried about her getting through the airport and onto a plane. My mother had restricted her months before to domestic flights only, and I feel relieved she is not in Zimbabwe or Tanzania or any of the other remote locales she previously frequented for work.

I realize that this Oxford scholar with a handful of degrees and a few languages in her repertoire couldn't possibly hold down a job right now. I forward the voicemail to Lex and Mom and promise to get her onto an airplane. I drive her to the airport amidst insane tales of police at her hotel at 2 a.m. the night before and moments with the prime minister during the day.

Just when I feel the truth coming into focus, it blurs. And I realize there's really only one truth now: I always thought her illness was bad, but now I know. It is terrible.

KIDS

We were all kids once. Although I guess Katherine didn't really get to be. But Judson, Tamara, and I, we were. And all of us were playful and giggly and in many ways the poster children for what it means to be a kid.

What did become of us?

Once we became ourselves, it was too late. We could never be just kids again.

L

LAUGHTER

I am always captivated by how much fire likes oxygen. That you can stack the wood as tight and dense as you want, but only when it tastes the air does it burn. That tiny space between the logs that lets the light in . . . it's the same for us. That little giggle that bubbles up, forces its way between the layers of grief and pain until the laughter is ignited like a flame and you can feel yourself breathing again.

I remember laughing a lot through both of these losses. I remember laughing at the wake as we put up photos of Judson and poured him champagne. I remember laughing with my brother the morning Tamara died regarding how the rabbis would feel about cremation.

I feel like I might be a terrible person to laugh in these sorts of moments.

But it turns out, I'm not alone. When I talk to Mom about laughing and loss, she tells me, "After your grandfather's death in Naples, the coroner called to report that 'Mr. Cowan has arrived home in his pyjamas.'"

She says she hung up and just burst into laughter.

She also tells me that after Tamara's death she booked an appointment with Tamara's therapist. Upon her arrival at his office, he said, "I can't help you now. I don't deal with grief."

I can't tell if the second story is funny or not. But I laugh anyway. I need to. And she needs to hear me laugh today.

LOVE

I feel like Tamara and I misunderstood each other. And I don't mean Tamara in the full throttle of her illness, I mean always. And not "misunderstood" in the small, semantic, bickering sibling kind of way (though we had that, too) but in a more fundamental sense.

Tamara loved me in the way that a lot of little sisters do: she copied me.

> *I like the sweatshirt. She buys the sweatshirt.*
> *I listen to good music. She steals my mixed tapes.*
> *I learn to play guitar. She goes out and buys a guitar.*
> *She makes friends with my friends, hangs out in my "spots,"*
>   *tells my stories from school before I get a chance to . . .*
> *. . . etc., etc., ad nauseam.*

It drove me crazy, and I just couldn't understand that this was love.

In Grade 7, I took Environmental Sciences in a moment when water was not talked about like gold and endangered species weren't pictured on the front of magazines and Al Gore hadn't made his documentary and people weren't scared. Not like they are now. And I was hooked.

I might have stuck with it all the way through to an actual career, but . . . Tamara. It became an obsession for my mini-me. She loved the subject matter and took easily to the science and details behind it. More than that, it was a place to force the dialogue with me, a place to compete with me, and it was in my wing of the school, with my teachers, in my space.

So I backed off environmental science. I told myself that when it wasn't my favourite teacher, Mrs. Bell, at the front of the room, I wasn't really that interested in it after all. I told myself that Tamara deserved something that was truly hers.

And I was convinced of that, that I was giving her something. But Tamara was angry at me. She was angry that I'd abandoned our "shared" passion. She felt betrayed. And it wouldn't be the last time she felt that. As she got sicker and sicker, she must have felt that I betrayed her more and more.

I loved Tamara in the way that a lot of big sisters do: I tried to protect her.

> She tells a lie. I call her out on it.
> She makes up a story. I make it OK with the teacher.
> She freaks out. I inform my mother.
> And I talk about her with my friends, our parents and siblings
>   and psychologists, and I ask about her mental health . . .
> . . . etc., etc., ad nauseam.

It drove her crazy, and she just couldn't understand that this was love.

LIES

In the months that follow Judson's death, I'm getting the space to process this loss. And the silence. No one mentions his name in front of me. People look awkward when I bring him up, especially if it's a funny story. People won't touch this issue. So it's like he doesn't exist.

It's. Way. Too. Much. Space. A giant Judson-sized hole. Judson: my first love, my first gay BFF, my best friend, that bitchy queen I know and love. His favourite saying was "I ain't your ho!" And when he was really worked up, "I ain't your ho, I ain't his ho, I am my oooowwwwwn ho." All arms and legs with giant blue eyes, a lopsided smile, and so far out of the closet he's not even going back in for the mittens he forgot—Judson was most definitely his own ho.

I'm filling this giant empty space with cocaine.

It has become a game I play. How often can I be high and get away with it? Who will figure it out first? How do I cover my tracks? I lie really well, and the only rule is that I can't get caught . . . so as it turns out, I am winning the game!

And by that, I mean I'm losing. Badly.

Because now it's been a year and a half and no one knows. My boss is totally oblivious, and my friends don't bug me about not coming out on the weekend. They think I'm just working through this loss. My boyfriend, Anthony, knows that something's wrong, but he's giving me space. He tiptoes around me. We don't eat meals together anymore. Sometimes (when I'm high) I burst through the door with a million things to say, and he sits and listens and puts whatever he's doing away. Other times (when I'm coming down) I come home and just growl at him and curl my lip, and he has learned to make himself busy.

I've been given so much space I'm falling through the cracks.

And I'm running out of money for the month, so I can't buy any more. I don't know if I can stop this by myself. But I've been lying for so long I can't tell the truth now. I need a reason to be clean. I just need a sign.

As I stumble through the door one day, I bark at Anthony, "Why wasn't the door locked?"

There's silence from upstairs and then his voice, "I ain't your ho."

He's right. In the moment that I realize that I am my own ho, a little piece of that Judson-sized hole is filled in and my last baggie of blow is flushed down the toilet.

LAST WORDS

November 10, 2016

> **LIZ**
> *Got your message last night. I'm directing my first movie right now and not done until mid next week. We will talk once I wrap. Lots of love.*

TAMARA
lots of love back!

November 13

TAMARA
How are you doing?
Sending you virtual hugs.

> **LIZ**
> *See text above!*

November 14

TAMARA
Why are you always so bitchy? It takes

*as much effort to send a virtual hug as
to say see text above. You are a pretty
crappy big sister who has offered almost
zero support through schizophrenia
diagnosis and hellish months of hospitals,
meds and side effects. I think a few
phone calls and texts this month is pretty
pathetic. We have never been close but
you could try.*

LIZ
Sorry you see it that way.

TAMARA
*I am sure it is just my
perspective. I know you have tried.
And I know you have amazing talents
and skills. I love you I just don't love
myself these days.*

LIZ:
*Awww honey. Know that you are loved.
Understand that we are all here for you,
albeit in different ways, and know that
it will just take time to build your own
self worth and your relationships back to
where you want and deserve them to be.
Please understand that I have spent 40
years building to what I have done in the
past few months. It won't help us grow if
I feel attacked at a time like this—I have
worked to be there for you and I'm sorry
if you feel like i have failed but there is
a lot between us that needs healing so*

getting a text like this puts us backwards when we have come so far since you started on your healing journey. Let's try and stay forward focused, open and positive and tell each other what we need (love) instead of pointing fingers (bitchy, crappy sister).

Be patient: with yourself, and with us.

Be gentle: on yourself and those trying to support you.

Be love: as often as possible to yourself and others—even when it's not easy.

All that patience, gentleness and love WILL come back to you in spades.

Now here's what I need: to go finish this movie knowing that you are OK!! xoxoxoxoxoxo

TAMARA
Thank you for the message I am proud of you. Go finish the movie and know that I love and admire you.

November 17

TAMARA
I hear you told mom you were stressed about our last exchange. I am sorry it

stressed you out. You are an amazing
talented person and super busy. I had no
right to pull on you. I hope you are good
and that your projects succeed beyond
your wildest dreams.

None of this matters anyway. I didn't call her back for three weeks before she died.

M

MATH.

A whole bunch of little things can add up to a big thing.

MIRROR

I see sisters everywhere.

Which is strange. Because I never saw us as sisters.

MIRAGE

When it happened, I thought I was seeing things. It is 1 a.m., maybe 1:30 a.m., over Christmas holidays, and I am walking from my friend's to my family home in Toronto. As I turn a corner, he steps out of the shadows. Well over 6 feet tall, a baseball cap and these impossibly long arms with a slight tilt to his head. I stop. My brain is reeling, and I have to remind myself to breathe. I can feel panic welling up inside me as he gets closer.

My feet are glued to the cement. I can see his smile—it is really him. I am actually confused for a moment—not yearning for the possibility of being confused—but actually unsure. And then he's there. Beside me.

It's Josh.

MOM

My mother invented a world for us. She built it, one tiny brick at a time. It started before I was even born. Mom wasn't supposed to have kids, or at least her body wasn't. She went on fertility drugs before she had me—Elizabeth (consecrated to God) Aimee (beloved) Levine.

Nearly four years later, by some sort of miracle, or maybe just the universe recognizing that she was the best mom ever, she had quadruplets.

Nothing slowed my mother down. Not even Katherine's death. She would have a child on her shoulder, one in her arms being fed, one being rocked in a car seat at her feet, and me, jumping around, singing, playing, vying for attention. And somehow she had enough for all of us. Not just for the things we needed, like food, or the things that were good for us, like hugs. She had room for everything that we needed and everything that we wanted and the things we didn't know we needed or wanted until she gave them to us.

After school, snacks would be on the table. My mom would take a cheese slicer and peel off long, thin strips of cheddar cheese for each of us and then pretend to read from them, like a letter. These imaginary notes were full of praise and support, and we all had to sit around the table and hear them before we could eat them with our slices of crisp green apple.

She wanted us to have it all—our house filled with games and toys and musical instruments and sporting equipment. Life was a whirl-wind of music lessons, sports games, summer camps, cottages. In the summer, she taught us to drive boats, swim, fish, and to love the out-of-doors. During the school year, she taught us to read, how to cook things, and to paint and draw and sing.

She transferred this same energy to the holidays. We celebrated Easter and Passover, we got chocolate eggs and matzo, we lit the menorah on Hanukkah, and decorated a tree for Christmas. And while it might seem strange to some, to her it was about choice and about experience. It was about what she believed and about what she loved to do, but also about what we would choose for ourselves. She was open to, and endlessly fascinated by, our choices.

And she was truly a momma bear—she would growl at those who slighted us. She went to every parent-teacher night, fought for us, circled around and got involved with our friends' parents, sniffed out where we were going and what we were doing. She encouraged our freedom and our sense of discovery but was happiest when the four of us were close to her, around the kitchen table.

With all of that, she was protecting us, her cubs. Protecting the sick-est or the weakest first. She was following her instincts. The instincts that birthed us, raised us, and raised us up. For all the frustration I may feel, I know this: She didn't know that it would hurt the stron-gest among us. She hoped it would save the weakest among us. And today I know that she feels she failed us.

But she didn't. When it came to Tamara, I gave up. She never did.

> To: Tamara, Allan, Alexis, Michael, Peter, Liz, Dr. G
> March 25, 2015
>
> Dear Tamara,
>
> All that any of us has wanted is to know you are FULLY engaged in a course of treatment that you can commit to, in order to really know the real value and benefits, or not.
>
> As a worried Mom, today, with your email to Dr. G., is the first somewhat easier breath I have taken knowing you have reached out once again to risk professional help.
>
> We have all been so alarmed by your recent thinking and actions that Allan and I knew that we HAD to sit down with you to beg you to try the route of professional help once more.
>
> I have been on this tortuous journey with you Tamara, all the way back to last fall with Dr. D and meeting you at your appointments. I know the meds are lousy but when you were on them briefly, just before your last birthday, everyone said that you were calmer and "better" when here at that time, but by Thanksgiving you had stopped them and seemed much more "off" as I have said to you.
>
> There are many different meds, and bodies do adjust a bit and/or being admitted to hospital to get the right medication for YOU, might be a possibility, and I would be right there with you.
>
> These are not easy words to write.
>
> You know you have had my support always, be it the 5,000 recent texts or 6,000 recent emails, the dinners, the drives, the celebrations, the films, the financial gifts, and my admiration for all of your many talents and caring qualities . . . . but your

reluctance to really deal with your health, beyond job search and exercise has created unpleasant exchanges and very scary behaviours and responses, and I do not believe we can all be "wrong."

There is not one member of this family or extended family who does not want to see you healthy, really healthy, not just functioning, and your suffering has been excruciatingly painful for me to watch, cause I am the mother!!!

Please, for yourself, first and foremost, but for all of us, move forward on all fronts with all the treatment you can, and however hard it is, we are all cheering for you, and are here for you!

*There is really nothing more I can say . . . .
. . . .*

Xo
Mom

For everything Mom has done for us, the only thing I want to do in return is make this feeling that she has failed go away. But I can't. And in fact, my very existence only serves to reinforce it.

MULTIPLES

Lex said, "When I was born, I was a quadruplet, but Katherine died when we were so young that I only really remember being a triplet."

He's not wrong. Since Katherine never came home from the hospital, they were always (to everyone's memory save my mother's, I'm sure) The Triplets.

After they were born, my father came home and told me their names: Katherine, Peter, Alexis, and Tamara. I am outraged. Why do I have to wait until *tomorrow* to know her name? I want to know now! I don't fully understand that her name *is* Tamara (not "tomorrow") until they all come home weeks later. Well, Peter, Alexis, and Tamara come home. But in this moment I'm not worried about who might be missing. I'm overwhelmed with newcomers. And I have a sister and she is tiny and perfect and here, now.

They have matching everything. There are three identical cribs lined up in the upstairs bedroom. Three high chairs at the kitchen table. Then there is the stroller, three babies long, which makes anyone on the street with a heart need to stop and peer in and comment. My home is filled with bins of cloth diapers (bless my mother) and dozens of plastic bottles and stacks of cloths and towels and bins and really anything that could be used to wipe down an infant (or in this case, three).

They move as a unit from the start. When one cries, they all cry. When one needs a diaper changed, they all need their diapers changed. And then it becomes conscious. When one doesn't get something they want, tears start, and then there is a subtle check-in with the other two. Then their little chins quiver in unison and each joins the chorus accordingly. They are learning to get what they want from the world, and they are learning it as three.

My parents work hard to ensure that I have "adult time," that I am unique from The Triplets. This generally comes in the form of "adult dinners" when The Triplets have been put to bed. Unbeknownst to my parents, this is the time The Triplets use to evolve their tiny unit to a full-fledged gang.

As we eat, we hear giggles and shrieks from upstairs, and Mom is comforted by this . . . until she isn't. We all arrive upstairs in time to discover the room trashed, covered in diapers and baby powder and diaper cream and toys and three impish faces with hair molded with diaper lotion and coloured with baby powder giggling maniacally. Spiked and studded, they truly are a tiny gang: rebels, warriors, risk takers.

We try again for adult dinner a few months later. As Mom, Dad, and I innocently eat dinner, The Triplets are upstairs plotting. The doorbell rings. Our neighbor stands awkwardly on the porch, apologizes for interrupting, and gestures to the driveway. Every toy that existed in The Triplets' third-floor bedroom is now in the driveway and on the car. Mom takes the stairs two at a time, and we enter just in time to see Tamara holding the screen from the window as Lex and Peter heave my antique rocking chair out and onto the front windshield of the car. They are not yet three years old.

Mom elevates the natural course of the triumvirate as only she can by wrapping me into it. It started when they were infants, with three matching outfits and one of a slight variation, but then when I am 12 she has the great idea to take a photo with me as Santa and The Triplets as reindeer for the Christmas card. This inspired moment leads to my ultimate terror. Mom takes over Halloween. From Santa and some reindeer to Donald Duck with Huey, Dewey, and Louie or Mary Poppins and the chimney sweeps, and it gets worse from there as the ideas become increasingly used and therefore limited. This haunts my preteen life because every cute boy I meet has a parent who is friends with my mother and so, inevitably, a Christmas photo of me and The Triplets on his fridge.

We all go to the same private school: matching uniforms, check. By the time The Triplets are 10, the boys have moved on to another school, but their friend group crosses over. Every birthday happens in tandem, of course. The boys and Tamara date one another's friends. Their graduations from high school and even university are celebrated together, and even as they become young adults they are still The Triplets to us.

When Tamara begins living in Europe for work and the boys are in Toronto, their shared birthday becomes a Toronto reunion of sorts. And as Tamara gets sick and eventually moves back to Toronto, the boys are by her side in their own ways.

And now, as I ask my mother how she wants to handle seating at Tamara's funeral, she is quick to reply, "I want The Triplets with me, one boy on either side."

A month after the funeral, my brother says to me, "When I was born I was a quadruplet, but Katherine died when we were so young that I only really remember being a triplet. Now that Tamara has died I don't know if I'm a twin or a quadruplet . . . but I know I'm not a triplet anymore."

MUSIC

Dad didn't ever talk about real things with us as kids, or as adults, for that matter. He didn't talk about Mom, or Katherine, or his relationships. He talked about "people" and "ideas" but not feelings. As I grew up, I learned that he talked about people and ideas for a living. I learned that he, like all of us, had a way of dealing with feelings, so that he could keep on living.

He wasn't particularly good at anything emotional. He also wasn't good at sports or computers or really anything that needed tools or equipment to execute. He referred to himself as "the builder of other people's chairs." He was good at that. He was great at the art of the deal and getting on an airplane.

Growing up, somehow I didn't understand how sensitive he was. I began to see what he was passionate about. He is passionate about art, literature, film, and, surprisingly, baseball. He shares that love with his father.

It is my first year at university, and I'm home for a hot minute. I have less than 48 hours in town, but a visit with Lex is a priority. We have been getting closer lately. So we meet for lunch, and as soon as we put in our orders my phone rings. It's Dad. I choose to ignore it. I will see him for dinner tomorrow.

Less than 30 seconds later, Lex's phone rings. It's Dad. Lex doesn't answer either. By the time Dad calls back on my line, we take pity on the dear old fellow and answer. He's out of breath and slightly panicked . . . "My TV isn't working," he says. "I can't see the Blue Jays game. You need to come here and fix it."

> *We tell him we have just met up for lunch.*
> *We tell we have just ordered.*
> *We tell him no.*
> *We tell him we are catching up.*
> *We finally suggest that he unplug the digital box from the wall*
> *and count to 30, then plug it back in and see if it works.*

And he tells us, "I gave you life! I paid for your university education! How can you do this to me?" And this is the most emotion I have ever been privy to from the man behind the newspaper at the break-fast table in my childhood memories.

So Lex and I put on our coats, cancel our order, jump in a cab, and arrive at Dad's home. We unplug the digital box, count to 30, plug it back in, and the game is back on. Dad then chooses to sacrifice the game by driving us each to our next appointments all the way across town. I know how passionate he is about baseball, but it takes a little longer to understand the bigger picture. To understand that he loves us even more than baseball. That this is just the way he knows how to express it.

As I become an adult, conversation with Dad turns to our shared love of the arts, and I begin to see how he is sensitive about external things like books or movies. I watch him watch and see the tears in his eyes, and I watch him fight for the projects he loves and the stories he wants realized. And I can connect to this.

But still, these moments are few and far between. For the most part, he and I share a cynical gallows humour and an ease with letting the small things go and burying the big things six feet deep.

And now, when I am forty, he tells me that after the divorce he used to drive by the house in tears knowing that we were inside with Mom. All this time I've accused him of being good at little more than hopping on an airplane whenever it suited him, or whenever something painful was going on.

I talk to him on the phone in the early hours of Friday morning right after Tamara's death, and we are both focused on practicalities. So when he calls me again, less than 24 hours later, on Saturday afternoon, I'm surprised.

"Have you read *The Globe and Mail* today?" he asks.

"Ummm, no, Dad, I'm just packing and heading home." I wonder what he's even thinking. Of course I haven't read the paper. I've had flights to cancel and flights to rebook and a universe to rotate because my sister just died! Surely it must be the same for him.

"There's a great article about Leonard Cohen's cantor and his final album," he tells me.

Leonard Cohen just died 11 days earlier, and I know that Dad is affected by this too, so I slow my disbelief. "I haven't read it yet, Dad, but it sounds interesting."

"You know his last album was all about death, right?" he asks me.

I'm cautious. "Yes, Dad."

"So I went to my office today and I went to the YouTubes and looked up his new album."

I'm quiet. It's not the moment to correct him about YouTube.

"I turned down the lights in my office and just listened to the album and cried. But I wasn't really crying for Leonard, you know."

"Yes, Dad. I know."

N

NAIVE

I wish I could attribute this adjective to myself.

NIGHTMARES

My nighttime brain is trying to understand the jump. How she got over the railing. How long she paused there, whether she did it one leg at a time,

> *if she stood,*
> *or sat,*
> *or slipped.*

Either way, every time she falls I wake up hard.

And sometimes I can hear her voice in my sleep.

NEW

Now, sometimes, it feels as though Lex and I have to get to know each other again. To talk about something other than her.

NAME DROPPER

My father has been accused of being a name dropper. When asked about it, he argues that he uses it to create comfort. The idea is that clients or potential clients have the sense that if others are well cared for by him, then they will be, too.

Tamara picked up this habit with vigor. Not because it made her clients have a sense of belonging, but because it allowed her to have one. It made the people around her feel important, and that made her feel important.

In her professional life, with those big names around her, she flourished, and this identity she created allowed her to be defiant. Her temper would flare up, and that would shift into her personal life, where she was most defiant with me. She wrote me a nasty note for Christmas 2012 after the family intervention. Even her suicide note, which had paragraphs dedicated to others in the family, had barely a line of text for me.

So I assumed she died hating me.

There's nothing I can do about this. No one in the family is quick to correct me on it. I have to make that OK. It has to be all right that I tried, and I fought, and I got exhausted. I had an extra decade of the battle under my belt. What she didn't understand is not her fault or mine.

But it's hard. I loved her, and it would help me to know that she loved me.

A year after her death, Scott Willis, the Easter Bunny, came to visit me. We talked about Tamara's propensity for name dropping. Scott acknowledged how bad it was and then told me, "It was always the worst when she was talking about you. She was so proud of you."

OPTIMIST

I just am.

OBVIOUS

I loved her. I always will.

ORDINARY

None of this, not one single piece of this story, makes me special.

OBITUARY

The brother of my best friend and business partner died recently. He was young and left behind three children. My friend wanted me to help with the eulogy. I read the pieces I fixed out loud to him and his mother over speakerphone.

It was very quiet when I finished reading.

Once the moment passed, his mom suggested we start a side business writing obits and eulogies.

Our tagline could be: "So good we make ourselves cry."

P

PICTURES

People take them to capture living moments. But they don't. They are static, dead, a flimsy carbon copy of a moment in time.

I can't remember that moment, the exact moment that picture—the one of Judson and me at the formal—was taken. We are both underage and holding beers. I am in a ridiculous crinoline dress and we are a foot and a half apart in height. We both look something more than happy; we look comfortable, at ease. We are not steeling ourselves for the next blow; we don't know that they come that way yet.

PUPPIES

It's week 3 of chemo. It's hard to say that it's "going well," but we are getting used to it.

I smuggle a puppy, Chloe, into the hospital today. I walk in the door with a squirming knapsack and a shit-eating grin on my face. Chloe snuggles up under the covers at Jud's feet. He says that she is warm, and it is a good couple of hours. We giggle a lot.

But after Josh takes Chloe home, Judson is quiet and withdrawn.

"Is it fucked up that Chloe made me sad?" he asks.

I shrug. "Why did she make you sad?"

"Because I miss it. Normal stuff. A warm dog curled up at the foot of my bed."

I remind him that he goes home tomorrow. That he will be back to normal stuff then. But I know I'm lying. I get it then. The new normal: impermanent, ephemeral, everything slipping away from him all the time.

It's like something is forever different now. There's no gravity in this existence, nothing to hold us here. Nothing to *hold* everything I care about. The new normal is about letting things go.

It's about how cool it is around his feet in the absence of Chloe's warm body.

PERFECT

I've known Paul for almost 20 years. For the past decade, he has been my source of sanity when I'm in Toronto, and we have formed traditions that meet both my need to escape the family home and his anxious penchant for one-on-one time perfectly. And our favourite tradition is Festivus with our friend Kendra—or as we know it, REAL Christmas—the one that starts when the torture of family Christmas is over.

Kendra plays host, and as soon as we get together we put on matching onesies (yes, we are almost 40) and pour scotch and roll joints. Then we share our crazy family Christmas stories—and with us, we mean literally crazy. Paul's mother has Alzheimer's, one of Kendra's family members is a heroin addict, and me . . . One brother is depressive, and my sister is psychotic with paranoid delusions.

We have been celebrating crazy-free Christmas together in one way or another for almost a decade, and for all the horrific stories we have shared and all the torturous moments we have rehashed together, Paul's only complaint is that he has never seen me cry.

"I mean, it's weird, Liz. Really?"

This year I'm not planning on going back to Toronto for Christmas for the first time EVER. I have never had a Christmas without my family, in our family home. I think it's time for me to have a Christmas my way, to start my own traditions, to get a break. But, as Lex is quick to quip, all that changes when my sister jumps.

It's late November, and the first person I call in Toronto is Paul.

He answers, and I sing out, "I'm coming home for Christmas after all . . ."

He is thrilled and jumps in with "Yay! I knew you couldn't stay away!"

". . . because my sister just killed herself."

For the first few seconds, I know he can't tell if I'm kidding or not. Once it lands, he's devastated, but his mission is clear: get a copy of *The Globe and Mail* with the obituary in it, meet me at the airport in 24 hours, feed me, take me to a quiet side street to smoke a joint, and take me to Kendra's. Simple. He's on it.

And true to his word, after I drag my bag off the luggage carousel, there is Paul. He wraps me in a giant hug and confesses, "I couldn't find a copy of the paper. I went to three places. Maybe we can stop on the way to Kendra's?"

"No problem." I shrug, exhausted. "Let's just grab some dinner."

"Damn," he confesses. "I was hoping that would make you cry . . ."

I grin—he's kidding.

We peel out of the airport, and it's clear he has a plan. He is determined to succeed in the rest of his mission, and before I know it the ride home from the airport is starting to feel like any other Christmas.

As we get close to the city, he tells me he has the perfect restaurant to take me to and he pulls on the steering wheel, and I grab the dashboard to steady myself as he crosses three lanes of traffic to take the exit. We are laughing when he pulls up to a stoplight. At least I am. And then I feel a shift. He's looking out his window, and his hands are over his mouth and there are tears in his eyes and all I can do is laugh . . . and nod.

Yup. This is the exact intersection she jumped into 90 hours ago. There is still police tape around the site, and a day or two later I will discover that there is a stain on the pavement that I don't want to look at too closely.

And Paul is crying. Full-on sobs. "I'm a terrible friend! I'm totally failing at this." And I giggle. And he hiccups. And then we are both howling.

The light has gone green and Paul drives ahead. We get to the restaurant and it's closed, and Paul cries again, and I laugh harder. "I'm the Worst. Friend. Ever," he says and puts his head in his hands. I assure him that he's not and that the next thing on his list is totally doable: a side street and a joint. He pops his glove box and smiles proudly as he takes out the joint. "I can totally do this." He pulls onto a side street, and we get out of the car. I light the joint. "You did it, Paul!" He grins and goes to lock the car, and sets off the car alarm, and it's SO LOUD and the street is so quiet and for the life of him, he cannot turn it off.

The week is full of more terrible things than I could have possibly imagined. Selecting funeral plots, measuring caskets and urns, picking up bloody evidence bags, packing up her apartment, proof-reading eulogies—all of it. And Paul is there for me through every second. Usually shaking his head in wonder that I'm still not in tears.

Don't you get it, Paul? I love that I don't cry with you.

The night before I leave, things finally seem to have settled and I'm sitting on the couch in Paul's apartment while he takes his air-conditioning unit out of the window frame. Josh missed the funeral, and finally I have a moment to text and ask him why.

JOSH
I'm not sure why. I just couldn't do it.
I'm sorry.

And for the first time since this crisis hit, I feel a wave of genuine emotion roll over me. It's Josh and Judson and Tamara and Katherine and my mother. It's all the things. And I can't help it. In this moment, there are tears in my eyes, and Paul notices . . .

I can see it on his face. He is finally going to get this moment. He is going to see me cry, he is going to get to make it OK, it's finally his turn! And in this overwhelming epiphany, Paul panics. He rips the air-conditioning unit from the wall, pulling a foot of plaster with it, and smashes it on the edge of his dining room table before dropping it explosively on the floor.

He looks up at me, and I laugh. And I laugh and I laugh and I laugh.

PARIS

Before I smuggled puppies into hospital rooms, I tried out my first, and what could have been my greatest, smuggling plan ever.

Judson was dating a girl named Joy. She was a model and going to Paris for fashion week. And Judson wanted to go so badly. And his parents were adamant that he would not.

He wanted to go to be with Joy, and we liked the romance of it. So we were in on the plan.

I can't remember the details of how we pulled it off, or who was involved beyond Karina and myself. I know the plan included borrowing a parent's car, sneaking a suitcase out the night before he left, lying to everyone about going to a cottage for a weekend, sleeping arrangements, parents who were out of town.

And we pulled it off. Mostly. Meaning we got Judson to Paris.

But it didn't end with giggles and high fives. It ended with all of us, and all our parents, at Judson's family dinner table with his parents livid and Judson on a flight home.

I've moderated my smuggling efforts. I know I do better with puppies than people.

Q

QUERY

We all poured years of our lives into helping Tamara. My mother more than anyone. And it's impossible to explain how hard it is— not the giving of the time or the energy, but doing so for someone who thinks you are the enemy.

We were all bombarded by accusations, constantly. At first it was about being mean, telling secrets, hiding things, sibling things. But the sicker she got, the tougher those accusations became. And by "tougher," I mean harder to understand, riddled with conspiracy. How does anyone answer an email like this?

> To: Liz
> Date: March 6, 2016
>
> Hi Liz,
>   . . . I went over to Woodlawn [Mom's house] tonight for dinner. I was told in advance to take back my card with the 10 weeks of lottery tickets if there were any plays or abuse.
>   Before I arrived there were strange emails, then when I got in the door she took Poppy down to be washed with purple towels, there were lots of pre-scripted lines but I ignored them all as I was happy to see Woodlawn and her. I really do love her. But although

I laughed off the weird emails and the purple towels ultimately she crossed a line I could not ignore—she fed me dinner with laxatives and then when I ran upstairs to use the washroom there was no toilet paper or kleenex anywhere. I jumped into a towel the only place to find any tissue was baby wipes in my old room which was converted for Wish and Atlas. I am afraid that was too obvious a play to ignore and seemed an inappropriate play from my mother. So with some reluctance I followed directions from the powers that be and asked for the 10 weeks of lottery tickets and my note back.

. . . I love Mom and will always be there for her and support her but they are right that I do need to draw the line re being poisoned.

The answer is: one doesn't. And when most of the emails looked like this, it meant that I was barely answering her at all.

QUACKS

I think we will spend the rest of our collective lives looking for an answer. The diagnosis didn't explain Tamara's suicide. Lex's chronology of events, while helpful in establishing a timeline, doesn't come close to the explanation that we all need. There needs to be a bad guy here. This must be someone's fault.

So in the month immediately following Tamara's death, I join my mother on her quest to find the bad guy (my words, not hers). We started with Tamara's shrink at Mount Sinai Hospital. I can't remember a single thing about him, specifically. But here's what I do remember:

His office was piled floor to ceiling with boxes and books and file folders. Shelves that reached beyond infinity with coloured files and scraps of paper hanging out. Messy, disorganized, and almost looming over us. My mother and Allan sat on the couch in front of him, and I sat in a chair to his left. I could hear them talking about the appointment Tamara missed on the Thursday before she died. I could hear a feeble explanation for why the hospital had not called us that day. About why, in fact, they didn't call us until a week later on Friday afternoon, an hour after we buried her. I can recall my mother laying out the timeline: Tamara's 11 a.m. missed group therapy session on Thursday, her 3:40 a.m. death on Friday, and the phone call at 5 p.m. a week later to say that she had missed her session. Too little, too late.

And then there is the conversation I have never heard before about a prescription for propranolol, an anti-anxiety drug. About how no one informed our family or Tamara's psychiatrist at the Centre for Addiction and Mental Health (CAMH) that it had been prescribed, and about how my mother found the five-day-old prescription bottle empty on the day Tamara jumped.

But the idea that my sister might have needed a bottle of anti-anxiety meds to take her leap of faith feels like background noise to me because I'm still floored by the idea that each of these coloured files and scraps of paper represents a life. And for all the details on phone calls and timing and prescription drugs it's clear to me: this man's office is a mirror of our mental health care system—and it's a wonder anyone could survive this experience.

Months later I go to see Tamara's shrink at CAMH, and this entire idea is reinforced: if you're not struggling with mental health issues when you get to this place, you sure will be by the time you leave. Looming, cement, dark, and imposing, this mental health centre has you check in between barred gates, and sends you to a lobby covered in signage about respect, violence, and mental health. The signage has, to my count, at least 15 different font choices and all the colours of the rainbow. Even I feel crazy here.

Her shrink at CAMH is kind. And smart. His office is clean and sparse. A good sign. But I learn nothing from this meeting. He doesn't "deal with grief" after all. And I'm giving up on answers. I go for dinner with Dad, and I ask him if he's worried about Peter. He tells me he doesn't know what to do for Peter. In fact, he says,

"With Tamara, when we all finally circled around her, it was the cure that killed her."

It's an answer and a scathing commentary on our mental health system.

And he's not wrong.

R

REMEMBER

I do. All the time.

REPEAT

They come like that. One blow after another.

RECALL

I don't lose my keys or my wallet, I never forget stuff I brought, or the stuff I need to bring home. I know memory is fragile. I know these recollections are framed, maintained, distorted, or forgotten. But I trust my mind. And my memory. And I'm usually right.

I needed to talk about those first few days with my mother. Enough time has passed that I think we can. I'm the only one home at the house in Toronto and the breakfast room is bright and cheery and we're sipping coffee and giggling, and I know this is a moment I can take with her.

As we get into the details: dissonance. I'm sure I was home Saturday night, that I stayed with Kendra, that I got to my mother on Sunday. Mom tells me I wasn't home until Tuesday. What would I have done all those days in between? We talked early Friday morning. Saturday, Sunday, Monday . . . three more days? I disagree with her. Strongly.

"No," she tells me. "I went to her apartment with the boys on Sunday, and you weren't here, and I remember because I thought it was so strange that they both wanted to look over her railing. I wrote it down in my journal. You weren't here until Tuesday."

I think it's strange that she wrote all this down in her journal. I don't think it's strange at all that the boys needed to look over the railing. I would need to do the same days later. And I still think I'm right. But I'm prepared to acquiesce that maybe, just maybe, I arrived Sunday night at Kendra's and came to the family home Monday morning. I do remember walking down the street in Vancouver on Saturday and Dad calling to tell me about Leonard Cohen. I remember I was walking home from the grocery store, so maybe I stayed here Saturday and flew Sunday? I was bargaining.

She still disagrees. Strongly. Her lips get tense. They form a thin line when she's frustrated. Especially if she's trying to hold it in.

We leave it like that, and I move the conversation forward, somewhere else.

Days later I lie in bed thinking about it all. Looking for clues, as I do. My email and calendar are no help; they clearly became a mess in that moment. I can't find a copy of the airline ticket. I go back and read the story about Paul that now lives under the title "Perfect."

And there it is.

My clue.

He was supposed to pick up the obituary the night he got me from the airport.

I checked. It was Monday that the obit ran. It was Monday that I flew to Toronto and stayed at Kendra's house. I got home to Mom on Tuesday.

RABBI

Religion and death. It's impossible to separate the two. And no matter how little religion may factor into your life, when your bloodline is the direct lineage of two of the twelve tribes of Israel and parts of your family are practicing Jews, then every death comes with a rabbi or three.

The morning that she died, Lex and I start talking about the funeral plans. And the first thing on the list is to organize the burial at the aforementioned family plot. We go to the cemetery with my mother, and it's the first time I've been back since we reburied Katherine and finally gave Great-Aunt Tillie a home.

My mother paces the plot anxiously and worries about how Tamara fits and if she should be cremated. Lex and I, problem solvers that we are, agree that cremation is the solution, to ensure that everyone who needs to can fit into the plot. Mom agrees, and we are decided until the religious fanatics get wind of it.

This leads to endless discussions with family members and the resident rabbi, who delivers the news to us, with absolute certainty, that Jews cannot be cremated or they will be trapped in a form of purgatory forever. With equal confidence, Lex, the lawyer, responds, "There is a precedent already set. We buried our other cremated sister here. She can join her twin in purgatory—and I guess you too, for letting us do it!" And with that he ends the discussion. Tamara is cremated and buried beside her identical twin sister. And I think we must be done with all this religious bullshit.

The day after the funeral, Mom decides to have what she is calling "a gathering." It's not a shiva (because she is not religious), it's not a wake (because that feels too celebratory), so it's a gathering.

As I exit my room on the day of said gathering, Mom is standing in the hallway on the second-floor landing, crying. "I can't go downstairs," she confesses. "That horrible Orthodox rabbi is sitting in the living room praying."

This is a problem I can solve. I head downstairs and introduce myself to the tall man in the tall hat and full robes who is rocking back and forth in my living room muttering to himself in Hebrew.

"Hi, I'm Liz."

He won't look at me or receive my handshake, and I remember he is not allowed to touch women.

"So, I think you might have to leave," I say. "I know it's all very well intentioned, but we are not a religious family and my mother is really not comfortable with you here."

"I'm here for your brother," he tells me.

"Well, my brother lives in a lovely apartment in Thornhill, Ontario, so if you want to support him, maybe you could go there. This is my mother's house and she is grieving the death of her daughter and she doesn't want you here."

At this point, the rabbi has gotten up from his seat and is standing in front of me. "If you tell me how your mother grieves, then perhaps I could support her in that."

So I look at the rabbi. And then I wrap my arms around him tight, shimmy my shoulders just a bit, and push my chest into him. And that's all it takes. Like vampires and garlic, this Orthodox rabbi and breasts.

My father later quips that he must have run home to take a scalding bath with an iron brush. All I know is that he wasn't upsetting my mother anymore.

S

STORY

Stories are the things we tell ourselves about our lives. They are shaped by how we approach life. It's about how we excavate them, the direction we dig and the parts we have the courage to uncover. It's about how these layers come together to reveal our truth.

I spent hours of my teenage life at Eliot's Bookshop in Toronto. It closed recently. I walked past it on a trip home and saw it boarded up with paper over the windows. I stopped and took a picture of it this way. In transition. Not alive but not yet completely gone from living memory. It's important to me now to hold things in this space. It was on Yonge Street just south of Bloor, and it had an upper level stacked floor to ceiling with dusty books down narrow aisles. I got lost in this space and in these stories. And I have stayed that way—lost and found in the stories around me.

SHORT

Tamara was always little. The shortest in the family by a good five inches at least. My mother called her Sweet-pea.

Being short made her cute. But it didn't make her small. She was little and loud. Fierce, even. She took up so much space, in fact, that it was easy to forget how small she was. Some days she seemed to loom over everything like a towering monolith.

On the day she jumped, my mother found a footstool pushed up against the balcony railing.

STAKES

I'm used to stories with endings, stories with stakes, stakes that I can control and manipulate. I can build towards an ending—adjusting characters, lines of dialogue, tweaking the tiniest visual cue in a scene to tell an audience, *You're almost through!*

But this story, the one mired in personal grief, is different. There is no end in sight. I don't know if it's because I can't see the end or because there just isn't one. These stories I'm writing are things I cling to, trying to not let go—to not be pushed over the ledge with her.

Despite the myriad fictional characters that populated Tamara's world, the stakes in that world were real—the stakes for her were real. So now the stakes are real for me too. And as I get closer to the end of the alphabet, I can feel the panic in all of this. I have seven letters left to cling to, and then, somehow, I'm going to have to let her go.

SHRAPNEL

Commonly defined as "small metal fragments that are thrown off by an exploding bomb, mine, shell, or other object."

It's Halloween, almost a year after Tamara's death, and I'm calling my mother just to check in. My brothers have been fighting, and she's worried about everyone's relationships. She is crying when she picks up the phone, and I don't know if it's the sound of my voice or if she was like this before.

"What's wrong, Mom?" Dumb question. It has been a dumb question for eleven months, but I keep asking it anyway.

She tells me that she has such a clear image of last year on this night because it was when they put our dog, Poppy, down. Tamara died so soon after that none of us had been to the house between the two losses, which meant Poppy was never really grieved. But Mom walked Poppy to the vet that day, so for her, the memory is crystal clear.

Mom tells me that she knew my youngest brother, Joshy, would be sad, so she invited Tamara over that Halloween to hang out with him and give out candy. She has a vivid recollection of turning back at the end of the driveway, seeing Josh and Tamara in tears, and going back to give Tamara a hug. Apparently, Tamara just hung on to her for dear life. At the time I guess Mom thought it was about Poppy. Maybe it was.

I let her story hang on the silent phone line between us for a moment. I listen to it for her. It's all I can do some days. And then I move on, and so does she. What am I doing for Halloween? How is work going? How are my travel plans coming? she asks. And then I ask her about my brothers.

She's upset that they're fighting. She's confused and frustrated with the choices Peter has made. She's exhausted: by Tamara, by trying to understand Peter, by all the things. We all are. I can tell she wants to talk about this but also that she doesn't have the energy to talk about it. None of us do.

I ask her about her brother, Uncle John. He was in to visit the weekend before. She tells me it was nice. She sounds tired. I know what's unspoken here. Uncle John and his wife didn't make it to Toronto for Tamara's funeral or for the tombstone unveiling only weeks before this visit.

She's in so much pain that it bleeds into everything we touch on today. I can hear it in her voice, in the turns of the conversation, and in how hard it is for me to make her laugh. By now I'm searching for something that will bring this conversation light: a laugh, even just a straightforward question of facts, anything except the uncomfortable silence and sadness.

There's a pause in the conversation. I can feel her ready to wrap it up.

"I just felt so sad for both of them today," she says.

"Oh, Mom . . ." I say. I'm tentative, but I have to ask. "Both of who? Tamara and Katherine?"

"No," she says.

"Tamara and Pete?" I can't quite hide the giggle in my voice as I ask.

And now she's fully laughing. "Tamara and POPPY!"

Right. Of course. The dog.

Sorry. Complicated family. Sometimes you've gotta ask.

SUICIDE

The act of taking one's own life. Synonyms: self-destruction, self-murder, self-slaughter.

> *If you receive this, I am likely dead or about to jump off my balcony with a silent prayer that I die quickly. This is my suicide note and an explanation of my delusional disorder from my perspective. Finding words that mean anything at this stage is difficult so the note below rambles at moments. I apologize for the long boring read.*

Tamara sends that email at almost 3:50 a.m. Toronto time, 12:50 a.m. Vancouver, and I am already in bed. My sister-in-law, Dawn, sees the email first. She doesn't, as I understand it, read all eleven thousand words before she calls Lex.

I wonder where her instincts came from in that moment. I don't think mine would have been so quick. I wouldn't have believed it at first. I would have had to read all of it, or at least most of it, before reacting.

So Dawn wakes Lex up in a hotel room in Ottawa, and he, I believe, calls Mom. Mom reads the opening paragraph and won't get around to reading the rest of it for over six months. She hands her Blackberry to my stepfather after reading the first line and runs for her car. My stepfather calls me from the house. My ringer is off, so it logs silently onto my home screen.

I almost never turn the phone off, just the ringer. That way, when I wake up in the morning all the messages that have landed overnight accumulate on my home lock screen. Upon waking, I can then assess the day in a single glance, and then, without opening email or checking voicemail, I can hop into the shower with a good sense of what awaits me when I step out. We all have our way. This is mine.

My brother sends me a text that says, *I love you. I'm getting on a flight.* I won't see the message for a couple of hours yet. Dawn sits down at the table and reads the rest of the letter.

My mother pulls her car up to Tamara's apartment building just behind the police. She throws the car into park and makes a run for the body. She calls me an hour later. My phone silently acknowledges the call, leaving me in peaceful oblivion.

So I am sound asleep in Vancouver when the crisis starts—innocent to all of this in a way, but also not. It's like I knew it in my sleep, I knew it in my bones, I'd known it forever . . .

I miss two more calls from home over the next couple of hours and one from my father. The silent buzzing of the messages accumulating is bringing me to the surface of my sleep, so when the phone rings again I look over at it. I see the email from Tamara, the text from Lex, and six missed calls. It's my mother's home line calling this time.

The phone call between Mom and me is less than two minutes long. I can't remember anything that was said. I only remember the feeling: like she was telling me something I already knew.

Lex is on a plane. I can't call Dad yet. I send a text to my three closest humans and get in my car, just to drive and to think and to be alone. I don't want to answer questions about this yet. I park five minutes away from my front door, and I open the email from Tamara.

I scroll through, and my first realization is how long it is. Eleven thousand words. Pages of jumbled, disoriented ramblings marked with sharp moments of clarity.

I have gone to my balcony a dozen times. I have gone to send this a hundred times. I do not know if I have the courage to attempt to end my life but I do not have the strength to keep living like this. Note 97% of suicide attempts fail and I am nervous this will fail and leave me paralyzed for life but I am miserable enough in my current life and fearful enough of becoming a life-long burden that I have to try. A huge part of me thinks I am crazy to try. I have chosen the most frightening method with the highest chance of success—jumping from my balcony railing. The majority of falls from more that 10 stories end in death. I have also chosen a time when there is no traffic so I do not fall on others but I fear falling on a balcony below and disturbing a neighbour rather than making it to the road. I hope and pray this succeeds. Yep! I've been debating this for over a month and I realize no one quite knows the horror of someone else's suicide contemplation. It was just a word to me and now I've spent weeks imagining all possible scenarios. Will I fall and just break my heels and legs or spine and be paralyzed? Who scrapes me off the sidewalk or the balcony below? Will I miss and somehow just hang on the balcony railing? How does Mom find out? Is it selfish to die or selfish to live?

How much pain will I have to endure? What is it like to fall such a distance? How much pain do I register for how long on impact?

She rambles on like this for a few pages and then . . .

I am not sure I ever formed relationships or attachments the way most other people in the world do. It is just something I never learned how to do. I think trapped in a web of lies and delusions that I never learned how to build trust. Therefore I suspect my passing will be a little life footnote for most.

My phone rings in my hand. It's France. I've been awake for 20 minutes, and I already know that the things burned into my brain will be more than a footnote.

TENSES

I struggle with them.

is/was

TRUMP

From: Tamara
Date: November 10, 2016

Family,
    With my delusional disorder I am supposed to double check anything that seems irrational or outside normal probabilities. Did the US really elect Trump to be the next President of the United States or am I imagining things again?

T

TRUTH

I don't know who Judson is anymore. He has become an idea.

I wrote him a letter after he died, and I tucked it into the dirt against his headstone a day or two after the unveiling. His mother brought it home from the cemetery in tears a week later. She told me to keep it. That it was important.

I've never opened that letter again. I don't want to know that I wrote it to the idea of him. I want to believe I wrote it to him, and that he read it, and that he understood.

TURTLE

It's been seven months, and my mother has enlisted my help on the continued cleaning out of Tamara's bedroom. I learned today that Tamara had adopted a sea turtle. His name is Shelby.

TRAJECTORY

She jumped on Thursday night or Friday morning, depending on which family member you talk to. But Monday night, when Paul drove me by her building, there was still police tape sectioning off a piece of the sidewalk and circular driveway.

I tried not to log it. Not to focus on the where, the trajectory, the wind speed, and how a body could be that far from the building.

At 3:40 a.m. on November 18, 2016, the weather was 7 or 8 degrees Celsius.

It was clear outside.

The humidity was 91 percent, and the wind was southwesterly at seven kilometers an hour.

I'm sure it felt much windier than that on the edge of a railing on the 29th floor.

I didn't go to her apartment until Wednesday. I went with my mother. Just her and me. By then I knew that Mom had gotten into the car and arrived just after the police. I knew that she had been there on that morning, in the dark. But when we visited, the police tape was gone, and I didn't look too hard at the sidewalk because

I didn't want to see the stained cement. We didn't have to walk over that area to get to the door.

Mom really wanted me to see her place and touch her things. She wanted to talk me through the new furniture she had bought for her and what I might want to take with me. She wanted me to open the balcony door; she encouraged it. I kept it as light as possible in the situation with her eyes on me, curious. I have a way of taking things in to be processed later. So I kept my moments on that balcony brief. But I had my iPhone in my hand, and I took pictures that I still keep. The gaze directly forward and the leap straight down.

I don't think Mom noticed me doing that.

Later, I couldn't correlate the balcony with the place the police tape had been. I couldn't understand the distance between here and there. It wasn't possible. And I wondered about the time in between.

I never went back to that apartment. I know Lex did a few times. I'm sure Mom did more than that. The apartment was emptied in a matter of weeks, and Tamara was buried in a beautiful cemetery that you'd think would appeal to my love of a long walk. But I don't visit Tamara there. She lived for years in the building that hosts the Toronto International Film Festival, Bell Lightbox, but I have taken back that space so I don't connect with her there either. And my family home can feel like a crypt sometimes with photos of her still all over the walls, but I don't feel her there either.

Instead, I go back to that cold piece of cement where the police tape was, and I sit on the ground with her. It's the only way I know how.

TAMARA

KIND

> To: Michael, Carol, Allan, Liz, Alexis, Peter
> Date: October 11, 2016

> Family,
>   A simple note to say in the spirit of Yom Kippur I have been reflecting on my life and I simply wanted to apologize for lies and health exaggerations which I know impacted all of you.
>   I also want to apologize for what a burden the current delusional disorder is and to thank in particular Mom for all her support. I am really struggling with akathisia and life meaning. I do love and admire each of you.

CRUEL

> To: BCC List
> Date: October 4, 2012

> Friends,
>   . . . You are the family I have always dreamed of having. One day I know I will achieve the same closeness

and understanding from my own all too busy relatives. In the meantime I return all the love even if I can not return all the messages individually before we climb.

With Love (Another word for what it is all about)
Tamara

When I asked Mom who this had been sent to she told me, "Everyone under the sun."

CONFUSED

To: Carol, Michael, Allan, Alexis, Peter, Liz
Date: April 1, 2015

Some facts about me:
   I am a triplet not a quadruplet. Always have been and always will be.
   I have never been and never will be an intelligence (or intelligent) asset of any kind.
   I do naturally make frequent spelling errors despite a sophisticated analysis and writing capacity. I think this is often rushing, sometimes a lack of focus and sometimes simply laziness. I do need to work on this.
   I have told lies and exaggerated my health. I have no idea why.
   I must be crazy.
   You are correct all of the "plays" I have been referring to must only have been in my head. I must really be crazy! I spent last night throwing pillows at my windows and crying and this morning curled up in the corner of my pool crying so any claim to sanity is long past!
   For any inaccuracies in this email I equally apologize.

I no longer know what is true or not. I feel like I live in a society that labels truth or unpleasant opinions even if not classified as insanity and that rewards lies and deceit. I believe in Darwin's theory of survival of the fittest. I would like to survive as I have real dreams and aspirations that go beyond being committed to a mental ward. So while I would like to see major changes in global systems in the interim survival dictates that I conform to the norms of our society. I think this email is my attempt to do that.

It is a confused email.

I am confused.

Tamara

TOMBSTONE

Mom has decided to buy a tombstone for the family plot. She wants to engrave something for Tamara and asks me to work out some ideas.

TAMARA ASHLEY LEVINE
Oct. 6, 1979–Nov. 18, 2016
Quadruplet
Well, she didn't hit
anyone on the way down.

TAMARA ASHLEY LEVINE
Oct. 6, 1979–Nov. 18, 2016
Quadruplet
Yup, she jumped.

TAMARA ASHLEY LEVINE
Oct. 6, 1979–Nov. 18, 2016
Quadruplet
Caring, compassionate, committed.

TAMARA ASHLEY LEVINE
Oct. 6, 1979–Nov. 18, 2016
Quadruplet
Finally, the screaming has stopped.

TAMARA ASHLEY LEVINE
Oct. 6, 1979–Nov. 18, 2016
Quadruplet
Impressive liar, challenging human.

TAMARA ASHLEY LEVINE
Oct. 6, 1979–Nov. 18, 2016
Quadruplet
Wearer of tinfoil hats.

TAMARA ASHLEY LEVINE
Oct. 6, 1979–Nov. 18, 2016
Quadruplet
Adopter of African children and sea turtles.

TAMARA ASHLEY LEVINE
Oct. 6, 1979–Nov. 18, 2016
Quadruplet
Psychotic with paranoid delusions.

TAMARA ASHLEY LEVINE
Oct. 6, 1979–Nov. 18, 2016
Quadruplet
Treasured daughter, loving sister,
intrepid explorer,
and caretaker of the world.

I sent Mom the last one. And now she wants to know if she should put her *own name* and Allan's on the headstone. I suggest that under the date of death she could just put, *coming soon!*

TEXTS

JUDSON
What's up buttercup?

        LIZ
        not much shithead. You?

JUDSON
grappling with my hangover.

        LIZ
        self-inflicted punishment. Well played.

JUDSON
haha

        LIZ
        Miss you!

JUDSON
ditto!

JUDSON
When you coming home?

LIZ
*Christmas. Soon! I'm booking my flights
this week.*

JUDSON
*you'd best be setting aside some time
for me.*

LIZ
I know! Are you at the condo yet or . . . ?

JUDSON
*Condo isn't ready until the spring.
Going to move back in with the rents
until then.*

LIZ
*Awesome!! You'll be around the corner
for the holidays.
Late-night. Game-on.*

JUDSON
GAME ON BITCHES!!!!!!

LIZ
*hey—so I land next Friday and leave on
the 28th. Just 10 days or so.*

JUDSON
*cool. I'm up north until the eve of, but
lets keep our xmas date and jewbouree!*

LIZ
Jewbouree!!!!!!

———————————

LIZ
the eagle has landed.

LIZ
hey. Never heard back from you once I landed. Guess you're up north. See you on xmas if we don't talk before!!!!!!

LIZ
where r u? I'm dying!!!
Please rescue me from family time (and my mom wants to give you a kiss)—oy.

LIZ
weird? I thought we had xmas date and jewbouree . . . should I be worried? Have I done something wrong?

LIZ
Flying home tmo. Sorry we didn't connect. Feeling more than a bit worried now to be honest. Please call.

JUDSON
sorry. Was out of commission. Call now if you can.

———————————

LIZ
*wow. Sad for you. The C word is scary.
know it will all be good but just want you
to know my thoughts are with you. (and
I'm gonna book a flight tmo so soon my
annoying self will actually BE with you
too!!!)*

JUDSON
No worries. Sure u can fly back?

LIZ
*nothing to do here anyways.
Might as well get in for the chemo party.*

JUDSON
haha. Sick.

JUDSON
feels good to laugh tho. Thx.

LIZ
I land Monday. How r u feeling?

JUDSON
like shit.

LIZ
hugs. Strength. I'm bringing you a gift.

JUDSON
?

LIZ
it's green and smells like weed.
Your mom said it would help.

JUDSON
omg. You rock—for that
and for dealing w my mother.

LIZ
yeah. Xmas next year –
you owe my momma a visit!!!

JUDSON
done and done.

JUDSON
here yet?

LIZ
just landed! Going to go home, dump
bags, say hi to mom and then walk over.

JUDSON
fyi—I'm looking a little tired/skinny.
Don't be freaked. Also, crazy fucking cold
here right now.

LIZ
hmmm . . . won't be and don't care
—can't wait to see you!!!!!!!!!!

———————————

LIZ
how is you today?

JUDSON
*feel great actually. The superdose takes
a couple days to recover from. But feel
much better now.*

LIZ
*awesome. even super!
up for a walk?*

JUDSON
*again, sick.
Totally up for something.*

LIZ
how about a movie.

JUDSON
perfect.

———————————

LIZ
*last night was good. Think you ate and
slept?*

JUDSON
*moved from the chair to the couch
sometime after you were gone. Slept
there all night. Feel good today.*

JUDSON
*thanks for being around so much these
past couple weeks.*

> **LIZ**
> *duh. Of course. How could I let you have
> all this fun without me? appt today?*

JUDSON
y. heading there now.

> **LIZ**
> *not even a little giggle?
> Sorry you have to get chemicals pumped
> through you.*

JUDSON
*remember the days when we paid for
that?*

> **LIZ**
> *who me??? hahaha
> Sadly, I do!*

> **LIZ**
> *how was it? Want company?*

JUDSON
*sucked. feel shitty. If you can handle it,
come over.*

> **LIZ**
> *be there in 15.*

JUDSON
*mom is annoying. Nowhere to get away
from her. Feeling tired. Very cold and
snowy outside.*

JUDSON
*coming down from up north early. Gonna
go straight to appt. Think you can handle
me after?*

> **LIZ**
> *I'll be in touch w the fam and see
> you at your place this eve.*

JUDSON
*Just in case the fam hasn't reached you:
they're going to keep me here a couple
days. Call the hospital room if you can't
get me 416-555-6269*

> **LIZ**
> *what's going on?*

JUDSON
*not sure.
Blood work says I'm getting better.
They are beating the cancer but I feel
like shit.*

> **LIZ**
> *hmmm good news. Bad news. Sleep it
> off. I'll call Josh and find a time to swing
> by later.*

JUDSON
please.

> **LIZ**
> *gonna come by in the early afternoon to*
> *see you.*

JUDSON
what time's your flight?

> **LIZ**
> *7ish*

JUDSON
cool.

> **LIZ**
> *I'll be back soon!*

JUDSON
remember that time when you snuck me
on that plane to Paris.

> **LIZ**
> *I remember.*

JUDSON
Thanks for doing that.

> **LIZ**
> *hey you. What's up?*

LIZ
Judson . . . ? worried

JOSH
*hey L, it's Josh. Judson back at hospital
same number—room 311 this time. Call
and I'll answer.*

LIZ
*hey. I know you can't talk right now and
probably aren't strong enough to text.
I talked to Josh tonight, again. I know
you were there, listening I know you're
reading texts when you can but find it
hard to respond—you don't have to. Just
know that I'm here.*

———————————————

LIZ
*it's so crazy to me that you're never going
to write back now.
I can't believe it, almost.*

U

URN

Poor Great-Aunt Tillie. Who would want to be stuck in that little thing?

UNVEILING

I'm not sure I've been to one of these before. I mean, we had a little "celebration" after Mom bought the plot and we put Great-Aunt Tillie and Katherine here, but it wasn't a real unveiling—they had both been dead for decades.

My nieces did not come to Tamara's funeral. They were too young. And if Poppy the dog hadn't died only weeks before, they might have been too young to understand death at all. And sometimes the older one has to remind her little sister, "Auntie Tamara isn't coming. She's dead now, like Poppy."

Now, 11 months later, Lex has decided that it's important that his girls come to the unveiling. He just needs to figure out how to explain it to them. So he talks about the cemetery like a park. A park we go to in order to remember the people we loved and have lost. And this morning, en route to the cemetery, he tells me he stops to get roses for the graves. That he gives two roses to each of his girls and explains that one is for each of his sisters/their aunts. One for Auntie Tamara and one for Aunt Katherine, who died before they were born.

The girls nod solemnly and take the roses. As they pull into the driveway, he says a small voice from the backseat says, "I need another rose, Daddy." My brother, ever patient, asks why. "For Poppy!" is the resounding reply.

As he lifts the girls out of the car, he gives them each an additional rose and recommends that they go find the perfect tree to remember Poppy and to leave the first of their now three roses there.

I'm driving Mom, so it's just the two of us in her car. She's relieved about that at this moment. Me, not so much. I'm holding my breath. Driving through this cemetery feels familiar but not comfortable. I'm starting to deeply understand the meaning of the term "family plot." I am sad for a flicker of a moment that Gammy and Gramps aren't buried here. I have to swallow hard. I wonder if the pain of the family lives here now, in this physical place. Like the sadness of it all is something that you could come back to and visit once a year.

We pull up near the plot, and Mom can't get out of the car. She can't do anything but fight her tears right now and twist a tissue in her fists. It's hard to talk, and I can already see the extended family noticing us. I get out of the car and go greet them for her.

It feels like it is taking forever to gather everyone at the graveside. The girls are having a walk around, the uncle with the walker is moving so slowly he might be moving backwards, some cousins or step-siblings can't find the right area of the cemetery, and my father is on the phone trying to direct them. And I'm standing here with Tamara's tombstone covered in a white cloth, and my mother shaking silently beside me.

As always for me, the actual ritualized event is a blur. I'm all surface so not sure of the details of what's happening, but I know my father says a few words, a Hebrew prayer is read by my brother Peter, there's a reading, a little talk, my stepsister-in-law reads a poem. And finally someone is lifting the cloth from the stone and it's quiet. Really quiet.

My mother steps forward and puts her flowers on both Katherine's grave and Tamara's.

TAMARA ASHLEY LEVINE
Oct. 6, 1979–Nov. 18, 2016
Quadruplet
Treasured Daughter, Beloved Sister
Intrepid Explorer.
Passionate, Compassionate, Caring.

The image of my mother standing at the foot of both her daughters' graves is one I know in the moment I see it that I will never forget. And I am reminded of Judson's father in the swirling snow nearly a dozen years before.

Mom comes back to stand beside me. Lean on me. She's coming apart. Lex gestures to his girls that they can now place their flowers on the graves. They take this very seriously and walk slowly and carefully place their flowers on each of the graves, one at a time.

And in the moment of quiet that follows this grand accomplishment, my niece begins to skip across the lawn into our waiting arms and announces in her loudest and proudest voice, "This is so much fun!"

U-TURN

I'm packed. I've been home so long I brought the car with me, so now I'm driving back to Vancouver alone. And leaving Toronto feels like another loss right now. All goodbyes feel like losing to me—it's something I've noticed. But maybe this can work. This new shape—the Judson-shaped hole in me. And the Tamara-shaped hole, the space I didn't even realize she took up until she was gone. Maybe there is a way to refill parts of them.

I'm looking for the clues just north of Toronto on a stretch of highway that burrows into the heart of the Canadian Shield. It is beyond depressing. It's hundreds of miles of jagged earth, looming pines, and rocky outcrops that could otherwise remind someone of cottage country, but to me, on this day, I am stunned by the sheer space of it all. The space between us. The spaces we need to travel to connect and become whole.

I'm heading home, but I have the sense of a journey. I don't have a fixed deadline. I could do the drive in as little as three days, or I could take two weeks. I think I'll see how I feel.

And I have been feeling. Not thinking for once.

I spend my first few hours driving away from Judson and crying about him. It's more than a decade overdue, and it hits me hard.

I'm not crying about the end but finally and honestly grieving the losses of him: I cry for the way he looked at me. I fight traffic north towards Sudbury and on to Thunder Bay, and I cry for our history, a story that would never be written. I cry for all the things I knew that I'd already started to forget: the sound of his voice, how the skin lay over the muscles in his forearms, how he went a perfect golden brown in the summer with soft blond hairs on his arms and legs, how he smelled like chlorine and sweat and a hint of Dolce & Gabbana.

I spend the next few hours crying about Tamara. For the first time I'm not crying for the tragedy of it all or for the horror of it. I'm crying for her. For how short her life was. For how much she had left to do, for how much she had yet to live, and how much she suffered in her time here.

I stop to fill the car with gas, and the kindness of the man who fills my tank has me in tears. I am so raw still. I stop crying for about 15 minutes at a time, but anything can set me off, from the Beach Boys song on the radio to the price of gas. I'm a mess.

For the first time in my life, I have no control over the tears that I'm shedding and no idea how to help myself. It's scary. And the only thing I can think of is *go through*. I resist this with every cell in my being. Why? Why pain and torture and hurt? Why can't I just ignore this and add it to my brief history of death? There must be a purpose or a point.

I'm clearly having an existential crisis. And I waver between striking pain and giggles over how ridiculous this all is.

I hurt.

I hurt from the inside out.

I lie on the bed in a dark hotel room that night and google the following: "crying, pain, loss, sadness, depression?"

I start my second day in a swirl of new language, ideas, and thoughts. It feels like a long time since I've spoken to anyone. It feels like a very long time to be alone in my own head. The road is eating away at me. I need to get out of Ontario, out of the dark, windless roads and into the sunshine of the prairies—as though passing that invisible line on the road will put me somewhere instead of this nowhere.

I can't look back.

But looking forward is like staring into the abyss.

I am haunted by grief on this drive. Not by the grief I have felt, or even the loss I have experienced, but by the idea of it: how vast it is, how dangerous it seems, and why I'm so compelled to go as far as I can. I'm tearing myself apart, and I'm doing it on purpose.

I've been thinking these thoughts for hours.

Go gently.

I need to stop driving immediately, but I feel like I could do this forever: wake up in a strange place, all alone, get in my car, and just be as ephemeral as this life. Just move forward towards nothing and from nothing. Live in the understanding that I've lost everything even in the moment that I have it all.

It's like present-tense nostalgia. Essentially, the happier I am, the sadder I am.

It's a fucking depressing idea.

I'm doing this to *get through*, and I've moved so many miles into it that something is forever different now. There's no gravity in this existence, nothing to hold me here. Nothing to hold everything I care about. The new normal is about letting things go.

So I've been letting things go for the last five hours with the warm wind whipping across my face. I have finally found a place where I can use the idea about the alphabet. I will risk feeling it, and freeing it, one letter at a time.

My alphabet isn't a history of death. It's a collection of the things that make up loss. It is about defining the abyss. It weighs it and it measures it and it looks for the edges, so I can break it down. The things we have lost.

Innocence.

The generic highway rest stop has a volunteer program offering free coffee. It's not bad. I sit and smoke a joint, brush off the ashes and gaze at the endless horizon. I'm almost through Manitoba. The air is starting to feel different.

I feel weaker and stronger and more disconnected and more connected than ever. I'm so far from everything and closer than I've ever been before.

I don't know what to do at the hotel. I'm in a small town I don't even know the name of. The only thing holding me to the world at this moment, ironically enough, is my iPhone. I text a couple of people, and I google: "grief and trauma?"

The next morning, my first thought is that I just want to get in my car and get back on the road and keep moving through these ideas and getting closer to home.

Then my phone bings.

It's Facebook, reminding me of some death-iversary or another. And I'm laughing: hysterically, tears rolling down my face, laughing until I'm crying. My head is buried in the pillow and my first thought is: *It is two hours until I have to check out, still barely 9 a.m. I could just lie here.* My second thought: *I could just go to the desk and extend my stay and lie here for 48 hours and tell no one.*

The third is less a thought and more a realization: *This is a luxury. Grief is a luxury. It's a luxury that I am privileged enough to take. And I'm going to. I'm taking a grief-cation in Nowheresville, Saskatchewan.*

The woman at the front desk is lovely. She extends my stay. We talk about things to do. It's not a long conversation, but it's a good distraction.

I head out from the hotel on a walk. It doesn't sound like there is actually much to do, but maybe just moving along with my thoughts is a way to start. It's a low-lying town, sad from some angles, but there are glimpses of something else here: the small white covered bridge against the brilliant blue sky and blazing sun looks like something out of a fairy tale, and somehow appropriate for this strange and impromptu holiday. As I walk I see more of them: a rusted orange metal bridge for cars over the river, a small red wooden bridge for pedestrians.

At the local coffee shop, I overhear a conversation on why the bridges here are covered. Apparently, the sloping roofs are so the snow can slide harmlessly off into the river. I also learn that wooden bridges that aren't covered only have a life span of 10 to 15 years.

Can inanimate objects have life spans? I guess so. Periods of time during which they exist.

My tears are slowing to hiccups.

I'm seeing it.

I'm understanding something on a visceral level. Somewhere beneath the grief there is a new kind of joy starting to bubble to the surface.

I walk back to my room and google: "joy and pain."

UNRAVEL

. . . It's a feeling. Like waiting for a sentence to begin or end.

VIOLENT

What it feels like on the inside.

VALIDATED

I needed it for so long, but now . . . It comes so close to the end of her life, and so close to the end of the alphabet. And it's not worth anything. Being right doesn't matter anymore.

> From: Allan
> To: Liz, Michael, Lex, Mom
> March 6, 2016
>
> To all:
> I feel the need to document the outrageous behaviour exhibited by Tamara at dinner that wrapped up a short time ago.
> Mom had invited Tamara for dinner since we hadn't seen her in a couple of weeks and we wanted to hear about her trip to Vancouver.
> All was quite normal before dinner, chit chat about things; Mom bathed Poppy and prepared dinner. Dinner was served, all normal, all 3 of us chowing down a great meal—salmon . . .
> There was a lively and warm discussion about Tamara's impending move, jobs, travel, Spain. All normal, so far.
> When Tamara had almost finished her meal, she excused herself to go to the bathroom (I knew what was coming since I have seen this play many times).

After about 10 minutes, she came down from the 3rd floor and had been transformed from Ms Jekyll to Ms Hyde: she launched into a furious, irrational rant accusing Mom of poisoning her (laxatives in the food), that Mom had served her a meal different from what we had eaten, that Mom was lying to her and that she would never come here again because Mom was part of the manipulation and conspiracy.

Among other "signs" of our participation in the conspiracy: we were accused of intentionally removing all the toilet paper from both of the third floor bathrooms and, in addition, that Mom had used a purple towel to dry Poppy.

Tamara was irrational and hysterical and left the house in a huff, having demanded the return of a loving letter that she had written recently to Mom. This behaviour is part of the "I love you; I hate you" mantra that Tamara frequently repeats; that kind of love she can shove!

Now, I am on a rant and I should end it here.

I wanted everyone to understand and appreciate what a toll this nastiness takes on everyone and how tragic it all is. I doubt anyone needs a reminder of how ill Tamara is.

Allan

WE

Plural pronoun, possessive, ours. Judson and I were a "we." Tamara and I were never a "we."

WEDDING

He did it, Jud.

Your little brother Josh—he really made it. Not just survived but is doing it happily. He bought a little place in Cabbagetown. It's cute. It used to be messy, but . . .

. . . then he met a girl.

And he liked this girl enough that he started working more hours so he could fly to Australia and stay with her for three months. And then she moved to Toronto.

And he proposed to her! And while you would have smacked him in the head for kneeling down in a rain puddle, you would have loved that he proposed over the holidays in the Distillery District in front of a giant, beautifully decorated tree.

Her name is Chloe, and she's wonderful and kind, and they're getting married in May, near the cabin, next to your tree. So you can be there, the best man.

X

It's about variables, about solving something. Trying to make the numbers balance out so that these losses have a value, something tangible, and aren't just an endless hollow absence. Even with the emotional pieces of them left scattered on the highway and the physical pieces of them buried six feet deep, there is still so much unresolved. And there are so many pieces of the formula yet untouched: the forgotten variables, the temporal flux, and the mystery of infinity.

The forgotten variables seem unimportant in the moment, but they're not. They matter because they carry value and, therefore, affect the outcome.

Like Poppy.

Poppy was dragged home by Lex on Remembrance Day from a puppy mill the first year all us kids had moved away to university. I think he felt my mother needed something else to care for. Of course, my mother was adamant that we were NOT keeping her. She could stay in the kennel while we all had family dinner, and then she was to be returned.

Lex spent dinner describing the horror of puppy mills to all of us. And my mother, who we all know has a soft spot for fragile creatures, began referring to her as a Remembrance Day poppy. By the time the table was cleared and the dishes done, my mom had Poppy wrapped in a blanket, cradled in her arms, and was singing her lullabies. Fifteen years she was with us, tearing up presents under the tree, bounding through the sprinkler in the summer, curled up on our laps during the news. Poppy died nineteen days before Tamara did, and this loss hasn't been factored into the equation at all.

Then there is the variable of time. The variable I wish I could affect. The one I want to speed up to see the end of. The thing in the way of the solution. Or maybe, the thing that IS the solution.

I saw Judson's mother for the first time in almost a decade today. It was mostly about morbid curiosity. How had she survived this? How would my mother survive this? What happens to grief (X) over time (Y)? Kathy tells me she is surfacing for the first time since Judson died a dozen years ago. My mind is instantly trying to do the math. If Judson died of cancer and it took his mother a dozen years to surface, and Tamara died by suicide, then it should take my mother . . . I can't figure it out—I don't know what value to put on suicide.

Maybe it's about how to encourage the transition, how to urge time forward, and I ask Kathy what makes it better. "Just hearing about him helps so much," she tells me. "It keeps him present and with us." She cries with me and thanks me for the good stories about him—she admits that people are alway reticent to talk about him, to bring up his name, for fear that it will upset her. "It does the opposite," she confesses. "It makes me happy."

And I realize that is true for me too. Telling stories about him makes me happy.

Perhaps I have a clue here. I'd like to do that for my mother, to tell a story or to let a positive memory of Tamara surface in the hopes of reducing the temporal framework exponentially. In the hopes of making her happy. And I wish I had more of those memories with Tamara, but they're hard for me to find. And if not me, then who? The actual loss is so extreme that with Mom, nobody ever talks about anything but the end.

There is no solution here for me. No answer.

Y

YOU

At the end of the day, it's all you have. You are alone.

YEAR

When people ask me about Tamara almost a year after her death, they want to know what we shared. But the more I get pushed on this issue, the less I can see of what we might have had. In the months following her death, I was quite convinced we shared nothing but a high school uniform, some hallway space, and a dinner table.

When I was young, I didn't want to share anything of mine with Tamara. I didn't want to share, and I didn't want her to even have her own copies of the stuff I had.

When Tamara died, I didn't want her stuff. My mother wants us to have everything. She is allocating small bits of her to each member of the family. She wants *everything* used. I am sent home to Vancouver with bath towels. When I return to Toronto, half-empty bottles of shampoo, conditioner, and body wash are mysteriously on my shelf. My sister-in-law is given piles of clothes and used makeup supplies that she may or may not ever use. I think most of us just throw those things out. They are just stuff. They don't connect me to her—there is nothing shared in half-empty shampoo bottles.

And after years of not wanting to share anything with her, I'm desperate for something we had together, something that would make us a "we," something good that I could tell my mother and something of hers and mine that I could hold on to. So I started looking for that shared thing. I searched backwards through emails and text messages. I emptied my box of old birthday and Christmas cards. I went through photographs and tried to find those places but I couldn't. And it reinforced my working theory—we had nothing.

Now it has been almost one year, and I'm cleaning out my bookshelf and I find a small travel bag that my mother gave me from Tamara months ago. Something I kept. Inside is a handful of jewelry I will probably never use, but in a curious moment of sorting and organizing, I really look at what's there. I can hear the blood rushing in my ears as soon as I find it. It's a ring. And then I have to find mine.

And now I'm sitting, stunned, on the edge of my bed, holding in my hand the totality of the only universe that we shared: two matching high school graduation rings.

Z

ZIPLOCK

Uncle Brian's best friend Lily from California could not make it to the funeral. So before we spread the ashes we took a small ziplock bag and a children's shovel and saved a scoop of him for her.

ZEPHYR

It's been over a year. I'm in the car on my way back to the Whistler Film Festival. It feels like yesterday and like a lifetime ago that we did this drive on the heels of her funeral. I am anxious about this moment. The memory of it.

France is driving my car and the conversation. Sometimes we are focused on one idea or one conversation for days on end. Other times we have six conversations on the go, all at varying stages that weave in out of our daily existence like the air we breathe. Today, she is talking about this book. She wants me to read it out loud to her. So I do. Every word. The window is open just a little bit, and I can feel the temperature dropping as we get farther north. I can feel my words escaping from the page, out the window, whipped away around the twists and turns. Like they're not contained there anymore. Like I can't trap them here in black and white to protect myself from them.

We arrive at our hotel in a whirlwind rush and unpack and dress and race to the first event of the festival and then the third and the fifth. My friend Charles joins France and me as we leave the screening of the film I produced, and my team jumps into a waiting car, but we, the three of us, decide to walk in the falling snow.

We walk across the village in the eerie muffled silence. We walk up the steps and away from the lights and the people and over the creek, and the snowflakes now are as big as I have ever seen them and the white is piling up on our heads and shoulders and the snow makes it seem brighter than it really is outside. And I look at my friends, laughing, snow-covered, heads tilted up with the light reflecting in their eyes.

I could watch them like this forever.

But I still remember. I remember all of it. And so everything feels different now. It's like going back. To innocence, but without it.

I wish I could share this moment with him, and with her.

And in so many ways, I am.

ACKNOWLEDGMENTS

With special thanks to my family for their bravery: to my dad for being my greatest fan, my mom for being my hero, and my brothers and sister-in-law for being the best allies a girl could ask for. To Josh and Kathy Glober for their unwavering support in this often personal and painful venture. To my soul sisters: brilliant illustrator Jax Smith for knowing me; and France Perras for seeing my heart, drawing these first stories out of me, and reading them all over and over and over again.

To Anthony Windle, Adrian Salpeter, and Robin Kester for being my readers, provocateurs, and champions for so long.

To Deborah Williams, Mary-Lynn Young, Paul Deadder, Kendra Reddy, Skye Matheson, Solveig Johannessen, Shawn Angelski, Jessica Boudreau, Nick Torokvei, Charles Officer, Mark Bernardi, and Kyra Sedgwick for their support throughout.

To my wonderful agent, Hilary McMahon, for seeing something in the infancy of my first brushstrokes and pushing me through this. To my brilliant editor, Laurie Grassi, for her patience with my process, her sage advice, and wonderfully dark sense of humour.

And, finally, to Robyn Daye, who has shown me what it means to be happy again.

ABOUT THE AUTHOR

Photograph by Robin Nielsen

LIZ LEVINE is an award-winning producer whose credits include Kyra Sedgwick's directorial debut, *Story of a Girl*, and Douglas Coupland's television series *Jpod*. She completed her Master of Journalism degree at the University of British Columbia and has written for the *National Post*, *The Walrus*, *Playback* magazine, and the *Vancouver Sun*. She divides her time between Toronto, Vancouver, and Los Angeles. Follow her on Twitter and Instagram **@thelizlevine.**